Children Praying
a
New Story

A Resource for Parents, Grandparents and Teachers

Michael Morwood

Children Praying a New Story
© Michael Morwood 2009

Kelmor Publishing
South Bend, Indiana. USA
www.kelmorpublishing.com

All Scripture quotations are from *The Jerusalem Bible.* Darton, Longman & Todd limited. London. 1966

Cover photo:
Star-Forming Region in the Carina Nebula.
Photo courtesy of NASA and STScI.

ISBN 978-0-615-27372-3

Printed in the United States by ECPrinting.com

Contents

Introduction

The twentieth century brought radical change to our understanding of the universe and our place in it. Before the 1920s, people knew little about the immensity of the Milky Way galaxy and nothing at all about the existence of other galaxies. In the second half of the century we learned about an expanding universe, about a Big Bang at the beginning of the universe and, thanks to the Hubble telescope, were able to see images of thousands and thousands of galaxies in one photo. We discovered our galaxy has billions of stars and that there are billions of other galaxies each with billions and billions of stars. Towards the end of the century scientists established that the universe has existed for approximately 13 billion years and that planet earth was formed about four and a half billion years ago. We now have scientific evidence to establish when life developed on this planet and we know that human life developed very, very late – billions of years after earth's beginning. We know that in those billions of years preceding the emergence of humankind there were major catastrophes that wiped out most life forms then in existence.

This understanding of the universe and our place in it is taken for granted by children today.[1] Most children will discover this understanding in the school library, in TV documentaries, in their homes, and in their classroom. The notable exception is in Christian fundamentalist circles where children are shielded from such "dangerous" ideas on the grounds that such thinking contradicts the Biblical account of creation and humankind.

---

1 "Children" throughout this book refers to pre-teen years.

Those of us now grounded in what some writers call the "new story" about the universe and our place in it look to leadership in our Christian communities to help us blend this new-found knowledge with our basic religious beliefs. We hope that children will be religiously educated in ways that acknowledge this mind-blowing scientific data when they learn about God, Jesus, Church, prayer and sacraments.

The hope we have is not easy to fulfil. There are many obstacles to overcome.

Our Scriptures and Christian doctrine are not shaped in this "new universe story" world-view. Our Christian imagination and thinking and language have consequently been locked into the worldview in which Scripture and doctrine took shape – with earth as the centre of creation and with heaven, the dwelling place of God, somewhere above it. Many Christians, including Church authority, consider fidelity to that imagination, thinking and language essential to being a Christian. This impacts significantly when parents, grandparents and educators attempt to engage children's understanding of God and prayer within a 21st century understanding of the cosmos. Many teachers in Catholic elementary schools will attest to the difficulty of juggling the desire to move in this direction with their professional obligation to teach a Church-approved Religious Education Syllabus proposing the "old story" be taught – a story about the first human beings emerging into a state of paradise and causing separation from God along with death, disruption and disaster by their disobedience.

If anyone who wants to help children pray followed such a syllabus unquestioningly, he or she would be locked into explaining humanity's basic relationship with God in terms of a story that is no longer believable. Children *know* the first human beings did not emerge into a state of paradise. Using the story of a "fall" from a state of paradise to build a religious understanding of how we are in relationship with God is like building a house on sand. It results in religious faith resting shakily on a story that was never meant to be a scientific explanation of the universe's beginning. To insist, as the *Catechism of the Catholic Church* does, that the biblical account of creation and a fall from a state of paradise "affirms a primeval event, a deed that took place at the beginning of the history of man" (# 390) is to ignore all the scientific evidence to the contrary. That is not a solid foundation on which to build religious belief.

The biblical notion of God is intrinsically tied to an understanding of a small, enclosed universe, with a flat earth at the centre and an all-powerful, over-seeing God who directs whatever happens here. The God of the Hebrews thinks, plans, reacts, keeps records, judges, intervenes, chooses, listens and punishes. This immensely powerful, all-knowing God, a localized heavenly overlord, is the product of human imagination operating in the worldview of the times. Yet, one of the first things any of us learned about God is that God is everywhere. Not just that God *can be* everywhere, but that God *is* everywhere, holding everything in existence. God, in Hebrew thought, could be "everywhere", but this notion of everywhere is not remotely like the "everywhere" of the universe as we know it today. We learnt that nothing can exist outside of God. When we bring our belief in an everywhere God to our understanding of today's universe, we realize we are not dealing with a deity who lives above us "in heaven" but a reality beyond anything we can imagine. The "new story" has the capacity to honor both God's immanence (God's closeness and accessibility) as well as God's transcendence (an unfathomable mystery beyond our words and images). It challenges us to change our thinking about a "God" who lives in the heavens.

Why, then, does Catholic Church leadership along with leadership in other Christian denominations insist we remain locked into outmoded thought patterns?

One reason is fear – fear that if we strayed from the story of paradise and a fall, we would "undermine the mystery of Christ" (*Catechism of the Catholic Church* #389). In other words, we would not know what to do with the traditional story of Jesus as someone who won back access to God and restored what Adam lost through his disobedience. Any questioning of that story would inevitably lead to questioning Christian doctrine based on belief in that story.

Another reason is that if the Church adopted a more universal, inclusive understanding of God's "everywhere" presence it would have to surrender its claims of exclusive access to God through Jesus. The irony is that "catholic" means universal and yet Catholic Church leadership and traditional Christian theology focus on God, not as a universal reality accessible to all, but as a reality that can only be accessed through Jesus and the Church Jesus is said to have founded. This narrow, confined understanding of "God" is hardly for God's sake, as if the Church were defending something basically important about God. No, the understanding is for the sake of the institutional Church. It gives the Church unique identity as the mediator of God's presence in the world.

Institutional religion clearly has much to gain by focusing on an elsewhere God rather than on God as a Divine Presence permeating everything that exists. Focus on an elsewhere God supports claims of exclusive access to God and the unique right to be called "the family" of God. Those claims are not possible when the focus shifts to God as a universal Presence. No one and no group can claim a monopoly on access to an everywhere God.

We need to appreciate these issues because we can find ourselves walking a tightrope when attempting to help children pray in ways that acknowledge the data of the "new story" about the universe in which we live, along with belief in a truly "everywhere" God.

The issue of how to interpret anew the role of Jesus will be outlined throughout this book. In the "new universe story" context we can tell the story of Jesus in a way that is faithful to his life and teaching – as the revealer of the Divine within all people.

This book was written with a particular readership in mind: parents, grandparents and educators who have found themselves on a roller-coaster personal faith journey in recent years, a journey on which they have found themselves confronting radical questions about who or what "God" is. It is inevitable that prayer then becomes a key issue. Does God listen? Does God need our prayer or our worship? Does God consider what we ask in prayer and decide whether to grant what we ask or not? Is prayer for God's sake – or for our sake? Is God somewhere else and prayer "goes" to wherever God is – or is God everywhere? What is prayer really all about? Should we compose and articulate prayers as if God were an elsewhere deity – or should we compose and articulate prayers in ways that affirm a Divine Presence in all places, at all times? If we adults have experienced a radical shift in our understanding about prayer – especially in not praying to an elsewhere Deity – how can we help children escape the religious thought patterns about prayer in which we were trapped for almost a lifetime?

The book is born from conversations with and the encouragement and promptings of adults who are wrestling with such questions and have been searching for something to help them pray with young children. This is not a text book, but hopefully it offers a platform on which adults can confidently stand as they walk hand in hand with the future Church while knowing that so much is different from what they learned as children.

It should be clearly understood and appreciated by readers that this book is not intended to change the way people think about their faith. It is a resource for people who are already engaged in that activity and are looking for ground on which to stand, ground that integrates faith and the contemporary worldview. Many teachers, for example, find themselves caught in an ambiguous situation: on the one hand, teaching the "faith" and, on the other hand, realising that so much could be and should be expressed differently – and better and more meaningfully. In response to the sometimes anguished question, "What can I do in a classroom when I am expected to teach the mandated RE curriculum as it is?" this author would say, "You can do a great deal."

The wonderful thing about Christian tradition is its many stories. It is just that some have been overlooked or ignored in favour of more dominant stories. It is important that adults who want to help children pray get to know the other stories and tell them alongside the stories that have dominated – in the name of fidelity to Christianity and a deeper appreciation of Jesus and his message. There is, for example, a dominant story about an elsewhere God; there is an even better story about an everywhere God. There is a dominant story about Jesus as connector to an elsewhere deity; there is an even better story about Jesus as the revealer of God-with-us in our living and loving. There is a dominant story about sacraments which emphasises dependence on men with special powers; there is an even better story about sacraments ritualising who we are. There is a dominant story about prayer reaching out to a listening God; there is a better story about prayer raising the mind and heart in awareness of a Divine Presence always with us. There is a dominant story about the institutional Church as the unique pathway to God; there is a far more truthful story about the Church being called to do what Jesus did – to reveal the sacred presence with all people in their everyday lives.

Let us immerse ourselves in these stories and bring balance to the imbalance we presently have.

We are caught between the old and the new, especially in terms of the worldview in which we articulate our religious beliefs. The good news is that those stories we have at our disposal to tell, the less dominant ones, blend wonderfully with today's worldview. They hold truths and insights that stand the test of time. This treasury of stories about God, Jesus, sacraments, Church and prayer has the capacity to engage us better with fundamental truths, and to make faith far more reasonable and meaningful in an age when everything is questioned. When this happens we find ourselves praying a "new story" about who we are in this immense universe, who we are in relationship with the mystery we call "God" and who we are in relationship with everyone and everything on this planet.

The best news about this "new story" is that while it shakes a lot of old ground, it has the capacity to bring Jesus and his teaching about God-with-us in our living and loving to centre stage and to engage our attention as never before. This is what makes "praying a new story" so necessary in changing times.

How might Jesus approach teaching children today?

Based on what we know of his preaching, we might expect the following:

- He would tell children about a God who is always close to them.

- He would encourage them to become aware of God's presence in their lives when they are kind and generous.

- He would affirm their goodness, again and again.

- He would urge them to name their good deeds as expressions of God's presence with them. Living *in* love and living *in* God go hand in hand.

- He would teach them to trust God. They must never be fearful of God.

- He would use today's understanding of nature and the universe and how God is present everywhere in his teaching.

- He would talk about a way of life grounded in being friend and neighbor to all.

- He would use story as his basic teaching method, stories drawn from nature and everyday life.

We can be sure that Jesus would not talk about "original sin" to children since he makes no mention of it in his preaching. Nor would he try to force adult concepts into young minds with the use of abstract and technical theological language. We can be sure that his language would be very simple, the language of everyday familiarity.

Jesus gives us solid foundations on which to build as we accompany children in the task of praying in a worldview unknown even to Jesus. This book seeks to build on these foundations and to bring the refreshing, freeing wisdom of Jesus to children in the 21st century.

Chapter One

God and the Wonderful World
of Young Children

At an early age children learn about the tooth fairy, Father Christmas and God. By the time they reach the age of six or seven (sometimes much earlier) they learn that the tooth fairy and Father Christmas do not exist. Belief in God continues, though, and inevitably that belief is couched in the same childish imagination that a child shaped belief in the tooth fairy and Father Christmas.

If we were to ask young children how they imagine the tooth fairy, Father Christmas or God, their responses might greatly surprise us. We may be surprised by the extent of their fertile imagination and the way they literalize what they imagine. Generally, what is imagined is real to the child. Remember, we are dealing with minds that have no problem with Santa Claus knowing how every child in the world behaves and visiting every house in the world in one night or with the tooth fairy knowing when a child has lost a tooth. Magic and mystery and wonderful possibilities can be as real as real can be for children at this age.

How does the tooth fairy know when the child has lost a tooth? How can Father Christmas visit every home in the world in one night? How does Father Christmas know whether a child has behaved or not? Three year olds generally are not bothered by such questions, even if they happen to ask them. They simply accept the magic of what the tooth fairy and Father Christmas can achieve – and the answers parents might give to such questions.

It is the same with God.

Children at this age are not capable of abstract, generalized thought. Their thinking is literal, concrete, specific, and very much grounded in "How does it affect me? Do I like it? Can I use it?" This is the age of "Why?" that drives parents crazy! Yet the child is not looking for in-depth technical answers. For example, if a child asks "Who is God?" he or she is not looking for a theological response. The question is not really about the nature of God; it is more about how this "God" affects me and will I like whatever it is.

This is a stage to provide children with stories and facts. Their capacity to absorb facts is phenomenal and should not be underestimated – especially if they are seeking information that helps them understand or be at ease with their world.

The unreality and literalness of a young child's thinking and imagination are crucial in the context of their religious development. A young child's experience of constantly hearing adult references to a God who acts (in the child's mind) like a very powerful male can shape life-long notions of a God who is to be feared or placated. It can also shape understanding that, like Santa Claus, God can do anything. Likewise, the experience of constantly hearing talk about a God "in heaven" can entrench notions of a distant deity, notions that will prove difficult to discard in later life. It can also lock a young mind into thinking that prayer is primarily about speaking to an elsewhere, distant God.

It is true that in many schools and homes, educators will instruct young children in the belief that "God is all around you," and that "God is in each one of us." Teachers sometimes say, "Oh, we always tell the children that God is everywhere and is always with them." Some parents and grandparents likewise exclaim, "Oh, I've left that elsewhere, up-in-the-sky God behind. I no longer believe all the theology that goes with it." However, when it comes to prayer, both in their own personal prayer and in helping children to pray, the prayers are often addressed *to* God, as if God were an elsewhere listening deity. This happens so frequently it needs to be noted as a major issue: adults say they have moved from notions of an elsewhere God, they believe they have moved, and yet the prayer patterns of speaking to a deity reveal the movement is not as simple as they might think. Lifelong patterns of prayer addressed to God are not easily broken. The transition requires rigorous discipline with language and a clear understanding of the principles on which to ground new patterns of prayer.

If we do not actively counterbalance the common notion of God as an elsewhere, overseeing deity (a notion prevalent in Christian theology, prayer and liturgy) with other alternatives for thinking about God, it is likely that a child's understanding of God will become arrested at the infantile notion of God as the Super Being in heaven who sees and knows all and controls all. Consequently, throughout life, prayer will focus on trying to make contact with an elsewhere God.

Many Christians never discard this childish notion of God as a Person in Heaven who knows everything about us, knows when we misbehave, and can answer millions of calls every hour. The early thought patterns and images

17

about God are so deeply ingrained that many adult Christians continue to believe this is what God is like. God can do anything.

So can Father Christmas for a three year old.

As much as we might wish to shield children from being exposed to the prevailing, traditional notions about God, many children by the age of five will already have acquired Father Christmas notions of God with its male language and belief in a Person who lives in a place called heaven, who is in control of everything and rewards people if they are good. This understanding is almost inevitable, despite the best efforts of parents who want to avoid it happening, because of the many influences in the child's life such as friends, relatives and exposure to a Christian community. Since this is the case, praying with them should attempt to redress the imbalance of the focus on God as an external agent, an elsewhere Deity.

Our primary task is to expand children's imagination about God beyond a Powerful Person in the sky and to establish in young minds that God is an everywhere, mysterious reality, close to us, and life-giving.

This is not an easy task and there are few resources to help the process. Go into any Christian bookstore and look through the section on children's prayer. It is rare to find even one book that does not lead children into talking to God as if God is a super being in the sky. Even the best-intentioned parents and teachers can slip into the trap of asking youngsters to draw what they think God looks like. Would these children ever be asked to draw what they think "gravity" or "energy" look like? Of course not. Yet even adults whose personal faith journey has moved them from images of God as a localized heavenly deity still use God language with children as if "God" can be drawn or be understood by them.

Our primary difficulty in helping children to pray is that we adults usually come to the task with our minds locked into a lifetime of influence by institutional religion and its theological teaching. How quickly we want them to learn about God, that God is good, that God watches over them, that God hears their prayers, that God is all powerful, that God sees all we do, that sin hurts God, that God is forgiving – and on and on. We are too eager to teach them the "truths" we have learned. All too often we "pour in" rather than "draw out". We need to reverse our process and to stop thinking that our primary task is to teach. Our primary task is to be attuned to the Divine Presence already here in children and to help them grow in awareness of this Presence.

Children up to the age of seven live very much in the now. The world is mystery and they have a wonderful sense of connection to the world around them. In this they mirror the experience of indigenous people in their sense of being connected to the earth. Indigenous spirituality reflects this connection. Western culture and the Christian religion have ruptured this sense of connection and the spirituality that accompanies it by placing God, the Divine Presence, in an elsewhere place called heaven. We adults have been steeped in this ruptured mentality and often unwittingly promote images of a distant God. In order to help children maintain their innate sense of connectedness we need to explore with them where and how they experience the Divine Presence in the here and now of daily life. We need to focus on their sense of wonder and their desire to explore the great mystery of life and what it means for them.

19

Talking about God with younger children (3-7 years)

When we engage the task of helping children pray in new ways, we must be very clear in our own minds what prayer is and what we are trying to achieve.

We need to be clear that prayer is not for God's sake, as if a listening deity either demands or needs our prayer. No, prayer is for the child's sake and has many worthwhile purposes: to develop a sense of security, a sense of being "at home" with the world, a sense of gratitude, a sense of bonding with family, and an opportunity to express what is "ticking over" in the child's mind and heart.

We need to focus on the classical Christian definition of prayer as "raising the mind and heart to God".

We want to nurture the child in the belief that God is truly everywhere.

We want to honor belief that the Spirit of God is vibrantly alive and coming to wonderful human expression in this child's life. We want the child to believe this wholeheartedly.

We want the child to explore the belief that everyone and everything is connected in this wonderful mystery we call "God".

Affirmation of God's presence everywhere, in all things, in all people, is the key to the counterbalance we seek to traditional prayer that addresses an elsewhere God. This presence can be affirmed in many ways. For example, we can ask children to name the people they love, their favorite objects, their pets, what they like in the garden or in the world around them or their friends. We can ask what they like about it and why. We can then affirm the goodness and value of what or who has been named – and affirm God's presence there.

The clue here is to converse with children on realities important to them rather than talking in abstract notions about a faraway God. While it is true there still remains a gap, a leap of faith, an abstract notion – that God is here present in ways that cannot be seen or touched and we are asking a child to believe this because we say so – any talk about God involves a similar leap. We are choosing to leap in favor of presence rather than distance, knowing that Jesus did precisely this when he spoke to people about the "kingdom" of God in their midst.

Children's Questions

This affirmation of God's gracious presence is the key to many of the questions children may raise, such as:

Q. "What is God like? Who is God?"

Remember, the child is not seeking a theological answer. The child wants to know how she or he fits in with this mysterious "God" he or she keeps hearing about. Our answers should be honest, clear and affirming, for example:

A. *We have no idea what God looks like. God does not look like you or me. God does not have a body. God is everywhere, like the air, or like the wind blowing. God is in everything because God is a Mysterious Presence* *holding everything in existence – all the plants, all the animals, all the hills and all the mountains, and every person. Nothing we see could exist without God being present – not me, not you, not this chair, not this table, not the flowers in the garden outside, not the mountains, not all the stars in the sky, nothing at all in all the universe. Everything needs God to be present in ways we cannot see.*

The best way we can know what God is like is when we love one another and care for one another because we believe that's when we can see the influence of God's presence among us. When I love you, God is loving through me. When you love me, God is loving through you. When Daddy and I love each other, God is loving in us. So, even though we cannot see God, we know God is always close to us. God is in all of us and when we love we are able to understand a little bit what God is really like.

And God loves you very dearly – because we all love you very dearly.

Q. "Can God see everything I do?"

A. *Some people speak of God as if God is like a Big Person in the sky who looks down over us. But God is not really like that. That is just a way people try to explain God because we cannot imagine what God is like. God is like the sunlight, like the wind or like a Spirit that breathes life into everything. God does not see the way we see or hear the way we hear. But God is always present. Nothing could exist without God being present. God is not watching you. It is not like that. It is much better. God gives you life by being always with you and in you.*

Q. "Can we hurt God?"

A. *No, you can never hurt God. When we do wrong we hurt other people. We hurt other people when we are selfish or cruel or say unkind things or do hurtful things. When we act like that we are not allowing God's presence to act in us. Jesus said that when we love and share and help one another we are better able to know the presence of God with us. So it is not God who gets hurt when people do bad things, it is other people who get hurt and that means we are not able to be happy with one another.*

Q. "Who is Jesus?"

A. *Jesus lived a long time ago and spent his life trying to help people believe that God was close to them in everything they did. He wanted people to be good to one another so that we would all see God's presence in people. He believed that everyone would be happier if they knew God was close to them. That is why we talk about Jesus: because he showed us that God is always close to us.*

Q. "Does God look after everyone?"

A. *No, it is not God's job to look after everyone. That's our job. God gives us life and we have to do the best we can with it by the way we care and help one another. So if we do not do our job, other people do not sense God's presence. That would be a great pity, wouldn't it?*

Q. "What do we go to Church for?"

A. *We go to Church to hear stories about God and how Jesus taught people to let God's loving presence shine in their lives through their good deeds. We go to be thankful for the good things we have in life – like you, and daddy, mommy, and all our family and friends. And we also go to show that we want to live the way Jesus taught people to live. If all people lived lovingly it would be a better world.*

Q. "My friend Louise was naughty today. Does God still love her?"

A. *We all make mistakes but our mistakes can never take us away from God. Nothing can ever take us away from God. If Louise did something naughty she should say sorry to whomever she hurt and try not to hurt them again. We have to show by what we do that God is always close to us and that means we should be good and kind to one another. Will you do that?*

Q. Following the death of a family member or a much loved pet: "Why did God let Natasha die?" or "What happens to people when they die?"

It is important with an issue like this that our response should reassure the child that the world is safe and good in the face of pain and loss. It should also correct any notion that God is a string-puller in earthly affairs.

There is another pertinent issue here also: the capacity of a young mind to absorb data. There is not only a fertile imagination operating, there is also fertile ground for absorbing information. The acquisition of language and the use of technology are prime examples. It is not uncommon for six year olds to know a lot more about DVD controls, I-Pods, mobile phones and computer programs than their grandparents! Some educational research suggests we should trust the open, unfiltered, minds of children to absorb data rather than stand back, as it were, and not want to impose too much information on them. This research suggests it is only the lack of life experience that prevents young children from organizing and classifying data. The situation we are discussing here – the death of a pet or someone known to the child – could well be an occasion to give relevant information and help the child assimilate it.

Most of us have probably been guilty of resorting to escapist, baby talk when talking to children of this age about death. It is interesting that talk usually degenerates to this level only when "God" comes into it. If we were talking to six year olds with no religious background, we would doubtless talk more naturally about death as an everyday phenomenon, not something to be feared. If, then, "God" is introduced as a factor in the situation, let us not seek escape into the dualistic, cozy talk of "with God in heaven" that is so familiar to us because we have been steeped in it since childhood. The challenge is to stay natural and to face the challenge of explaining where "God" fits in, to state what we believe about God and that God is not the cause of death.

If the child's questioning shifts to what happens to us when we die, again, state clearly what you believe, but also talk about what other people believe. The child will surely pick up other beliefs and it will help them in the assimilating process to know there are varying opinions rather than being confused by people contradicting one another.

If the child is familiar (make sure your children are sometime!) with the life cycle of a butterfly – the transformation from caterpillar to cocoon to emergence as a butterfly – this beautiful example from nature can be used in the context of death and what lies beyond.

A. *I do not know what happens after death. No one really knows. But we believe that when life finishes here, another life starts. It is something like what we saw when the caterpillar changed into a butterfly, only we cannot see the change. We believe that what happens is very, very beautiful and wonderful. We have nothing to fear. We will be very happy. It will be another way of living in God.*

Bedtime Prayer

Night prayer could come under the heading, "The most peaceful way to end a day." It is a time for a young child to intuit that all is right with the world and that he or she is loved unconditionally. The faith needs of a child aged between three and seven are consistent with basic human needs: to be accepted, to be approved, to belong, to experience consistency, to know significant people in one's life can be trusted and that the world is a safe place. All talk about God should be totally free from fear. Night prayer is a precious time for bonding between parents and child, a bonding that is strengthened by interest, closeness and assurance. The lead-in questions here are suggestions for ways to converse with the child. This conversation can then lead easily into prayer that gives thanks, encourages, and consistently affirms God's presence at all times.

What happened today that you are happy about?

What did you like about today?

Who was nice to you today?

To whom were you nice?

What did you learn?

Did anything happen today that is worrying you?

What did you see today that you really liked?

Is there someone who needs special help?

Of all that happened today, what are you most thankful for?

Hold hands.

Ω: Night Prayer

We give thanks that Mrs McKenna gave you some candy.

We give thanks for the beautiful flower you saw – and the butterfly on it.

We give thanks for meeting Mary and Jane.

We give thanks for Daddy going to work everyday for us.

And mummy, too, OK!

And John and Samantha – and for everything they learned at school today.

What else? Yes, for your friend Robert, and for Auntie Jane.

And let us pray quietly now for your friend Peter who lost his pet dog.

(Include 10-15 seconds of quiet prayer)

Conclude with:

We give thanks most of all that we are loved by our family and friends and that God is with us always, present in our love for each other.

This pattern of affirming God's presence everywhere, linking daily events in the child's life with that presence and naming the connection is a solid foundation on which to build when other topics arise in the evening prayer time.

Meal time

"Grace" before meals is an opportunity to share how we are "graced" and to express how truly thankful we are. One way of doing this is to ask everyone present at the meal:

For what do you particularly want to give thanks as we gather for this meal? Let each person share.

The prayer that follows this sharing need not be a formal prayer like the "Grace Before Meals" which everyone recites together. If adults take the lead and over the years spontaneously pray along the lines in the example below, children will eventually be able to compose prayers in the same fashion – and be able to take the lead in praying at meal times.

The structure is quite simple: name some things for which

"we give thanks"; name some things "we are mindful of"; affirm God's presence; and present some challenge. For example:

Ω: Prayer before a meal

We give thanks for the way the Divine Presence is active in our lives and in all that we have just shared.

We give thanks for the food we are about to eat.

We eat mindful of the earth that provides us with food and nourishment and our need to care for the earth.

We eat mindful of God's presence in all things and in all people. We give thanks for who we are as family.

May our meals always remind us of the blessings we have in life and our call to be generous to others.

Let us enjoy this time together.

Amen!

The line, *"Let us enjoy this time together"* could become the regular cue for everyone to say *"Amen"*.

The model of prayer suggested in these pages is based on Jesus' ministry with people. He affirmed people. He brought their attention to God's presence with them. He helped them "connect" in their minds the link between their everyday living and living in God. He helped them "name" the sacred encounters: in visiting, in caring, in being generous, in reaching out to others. He helped people to recognize God's presence with them in the ordinary and the mundane. He tried to set people free from fear of the unknowable Mystery. He wanted them to be free of all notions of being distant from God and of having to win or earn God's love.

The prayer we want to model will avoid addressing God. This is a deliberate counterbalance to the common perception that the importance of prayer is speaking to an elsewhere God. We want to immerse children in the awareness and the belief that they are living IN the wonderful reality we call "God" – and that this reality can be encountered every day, every moment of their lives.

Chapter Two

School Days: What "Story" About God Will We Tell?

Up to the age of seven or thereabouts, children's learning focuses on gathering information and working out how to use that information. Children's thinking at this stage of life is typically specific and they find it difficult to generalize. About the age of seven children begin a significant development in mental capabilities that impinges on faith awareness which lasts until the early teens: they develop the skill of using experience to judge reality. This does not mean their judgment and grasp of reality are accurate or true – heaven, for example, could be conceived as a gigantic birthday party with free ice-cream for ever and ever. But it does mean children are more capable of asking whether something is real or not. During their years at elementary school they will become more aware of the world around them and more aware of diversity in cultures, ethnic groups and religions. This heightened awareness will lead them to develop an appreciation of cause and effect. Their writing and speaking skills will demonstrate their developing ability to handle more complex thinking as they reason and enquire about topics and issues. They will develop the capacity to appreciate another person's point of view.

Faith development in these years mirrors a growing child's need to belong. It brings a sense of belonging to a

31

group, a Church, a particular religion. It is the time when children learn about their Christian faith. But just how that learning should take place in these years is crucial because the shift that children are undergoing at this stage of life is monumental. In a sense they are being "brought out" of the world of mystery in which they were at home. Their sense of oneness with everything around them in the here and now is undergoing dramatic change. They are learning about differences and divisions among people and groups and religions.

Good educators will be aware of the need to balance the black and white attitudes that can develop in children at this stage of development.

It is right at this crucial stage that institutional religion seeks to teach children its basic beliefs. However, this is definitely not the time for teaching complex theological concepts, not even when this is offered in terms of giving children a "solid grounding in the faith". This is not the time for teaching the catechism – as happened to many parents and grandparents. It is a time for stories, a time to learn about heroes and heroines, about the triumph of good over evil, about Jesus who loved and helped people, about a God to be trusted, about belonging.

There is a long tradition in the Roman Catholic Church, in particular, of educating children in the faith at this early age. However, Roman Catholicism is not alone in introducing children to complex faith ideas well before they have the capacity to understand or appreciate the questions and issues which shaped aspects of belief in the first place. As a consequence, most Christian children learn answers and accept as a picture of reality the mythical and metaphorical language and images that are meant to point to mysteries beyond our images and language. They are not of an age to distinguish reality from what is a faith perspective or conjecture.

In formal religious education for children, adult concepts are generally simplified for children's minds. All too often the end product of this process is theological literalism – when myth and mystery and complex theological notions are reduced to literal belief that the mind can handle. This starts at an early age in Christian religious education and often lasts a lifetime or well into adult life, as many of us can attest. This is something we want to avoid happening but the challenge to change this practice effectively is daunting. Firstly, because the Catholic education system and other Christian religious education systems are so immersed in the practice, as we shall see. Secondly, because most adult Christians have been steeped in theological literalism from their own childhood days and find it extremely difficult to move away from it. For many adults, the movement required seems to be a denial of the faith they learned so well and have carried with them throughout life.

The prevailing system of early faith education backfires when it locks children into literal thinking on faith issues that should *not* be taught as if they were factual. It backfires later in life when, as adults, people rightly discard the literal thinking. The classic example is the story of the "fall" in the Garden of Eden. When many adult Christians discover that the human species did not emerge into a state of paradise, they reject the entire system of belief based on belief in an actual "fall" at the beginning of the human species. Many even think they have been deceived. They reason that their teachers and Church leaders surely would have known there was no such place as "paradise". This often sets up a domino effect where other aspects of belief are questioned and found wanting because they, too, can no longer be given literal, unquestioned credence the way people were taught to believe as children.

If we want to avoid the adult abandonment of Christian faith happening in the future as rapidly and as widespread as it is occurring now, we ourselves need to be attuned to how theological literalism is embedded in the faith education of children and be alert to ways to counterbalance it.

Take, for example, these statements of faith from an authorized Catholic Religious Education resource for elementary schools.[2] They serve to illustrate how familiar religious concepts and language so often handed onto young minds as factual, need far more analysis and examination than most of us might ever have realized. What follows here highlights the broader issue of what we as adults believe and what language and imagery we can use with children if we find that our own thinking and imagery has shifted. These faith statements are presented to help readers review their own thinking on some of these important topics.

"Jesus ascended into heaven"

"Heaven" is a word that points to a mystery beyond our knowing. It is certainly not a place somewhere. If we

---

2 The quoted statements are from the *Theological Overview* for Catholic Religious Education in the Archdiocese of Melbourne, Australia. The Overview is in the Teachers' Companion for the *To Know, Worship and Love* series for elementary grades. James Goold House Publications. Melbourne. General Editor P J Elliott. 2nd edition 2005

speak about "heaven", inevitably children will ask what "heaven" is and what it is like. How do we respond? A familiar response would be along the lines: "Heaven is where God lives. All good people go there when they die and they are happy for ever and ever." The next question from a child will often be, "Where is heaven?" A lifetime of Church language, images and teaching almost impels many adults to look upwards and speak in terms of a place somewhere else where God lives and watches over the world. Doing this continues the outmoded imagery, language and teaching about an elsewhere deity instead of coming to terms with the belief that God is "everywhere".

We need to be clear in our own minds that if by "heaven" we mean that place where "God lives", then heaven is everywhere. And we also need to be clear about the implications that flow from this apparently simple shift in emphasis. Make no mistake; it entails a significant shift in our thinking and imagination about death, including the death of Jesus. Death does not bring about a journey to another place where God really lives. Rather, death is a transformation of existence *in* the Divine Presence.

Traditional Christian language about Jesus "ascending into heaven" is a prime example of the theological literalism that needs to be exposed. In early school years children hear and read about Jesus "going back to his Father in heaven." Later, for grades 5 and 6 the "up" language is more explicit: "Jesus ascended into heaven to prepare a place for us." The pity is that being trapped into theological literalism starts so innocently – with the seemingly good news of a place prepared for all good people in "heaven".

One of the unfortunate effects of such theological literalism is that it grounds belief in an elsewhere God very early in Christian education. It also demands belief in a physical body ascending somewhere. This is a classic case of building belief on literalism (which ultimately becomes unbelievable to thinking adults in the 21st century) instead of honoring and giving respect to the mystery of death and dying into the presence of an everywhere God.

"The family of God"

Do we want to establish in young minds the belief that members of the Catholic Church have a monopoly on relationship with God? Are only Catholics or Christians "God's family"? Do we want to give children the impression that God plays favorites? If we want to highlight for children God's presence with all people in their living and loving, we need to be alert to statements such as, "The Church is the people of God", or "When we were baptized we were given God's life" or "At Baptism we are welcomed into God's family, the Church". We need to balance such statements by using language that avoids the elitist monopolizing of access to God. We need to focus instead on awareness of who we are. For example, instead of leading children to think that Baptism brings God's presence, we could tell them that Baptism is a ceremony that makes us more aware that we all share God's presence. We could tell them that all human beings are like a family with many relations including Jews and Moslems and Buddhists and members of other religions. We all share God's presence – even people with no religion at all.

If we do not attempt this balance, children will be nurtured into and will continue the religious divisiveness of an "Us and Them" mentality. If we do attempt the balance, we have a greater hope of nurturing children into a sense of a world community bonded in and through God's presence.

"The Body and Blood of Jesus"

When children in Prep/Kindergarten and grades 1-2 are taught that "Jesus' Body and Blood are given to us in Communion," it is hardly surprising that they get locked into life-time confusion about "body and blood" language. It is inevitable that confusion about Jesus' presence being a physical presence deepens when the words "really and truly" accompany the phrase, "body and blood". The words have been indelibly embedded in the minds of most Catholics from an early age: "really and truly the body and blood of Jesus." It comes as a surprise to most Catholics, including RE teachers and even members of the clergy and the hierarchy, that early Christian tradition held that the consecrated bread is actually a sacramental/ spiritual presence and not a physical presence of Jesus. St Augustine, writing about sixteen hundred years ago, was quite explicit on this. Commenting on Jesus' words, "This is my body", Augustine has Jesus saying, (emphasis added)

> You are to understand what I have said *spiritually*.
>
> You will not eat this body that you see ....
>
> A *sacrament* is what I have given to you;
>
> Understood *spiritually*, it will give you life.

Even if it is necessary to celebrate ... visibly,

It should be understood invisibly.[3]

It is significant that when Augustine instructed newcomers to Christianity about the Communion formula, "The Body of Christ." "Amen", he did not focus on belief in a physical presence of Jesus in the consecrated bread. His focus is emphasized here:

You receive *your mystery*;

You reply "Amen"

to that which you are...

Be what you see,

and *receive what you are.*[4]

Confusion and a change of emphasis occurred in the eleventh century when Berangarius of Tours was forced by Church authority to change his teaching about a "sacramental presence" and to teach that the consecrated bread is "not merely a sacrament" but is the "true body" of Jesus "physically and not merely sacramentally" touched and broken by the priest.

This focus on the consecrated bread as a physical presence intensified in the Reformation period when the Catholic Church, desperate to counteract Protestant teaching about the Eucharist understood symbolically, focused strongly on "really and truly", "real presence" language and on the Catholic priesthood alone being capable of bringing Jesus to the altar.

---

3 Commentary on John. 27.5 PL 35 col.1617
4 Sermon 272

This focus persists and is still presented today as if it is the only tradition in the Church.

Early in the twentieth century when Pius X allowed children to receive communion, it was inevitable that the practice would be accompanied by strict adherence to "really and truly the body and blood of Jesus" language. For over a century now, Roman Catholic children have been exposed to such theological concepts and language despite the fact that their young minds cannot appreciate or deal with the subtle distinction between a sacramental/spiritual presence and a physical presence. Doubtless this was done in the hope that once learned, the belief would never be questioned.

There are other ways and another story, as we shall see presently, that are far more faithful to Jesus and his actions the night before he died that avoid this pitfall of placing the emphasis in Eucharistic teaching on the physical objects and that avoid using literalist, confusing, and misleading language.

"Mary, the mother of God"

This is a theological notion that great minds have argued about at length for many centuries. The statement that "Mary is the Mother of God" requires very nuanced distinctions because on face value it is meaningless to suggest that a human person can mother the reality we call "God". Most teachers in elementary schools would not feel competent to address the subtle theological problems involved in asserting that "Mary is the Mother of God", so why are they asked to teach this to children? It is not fair to teachers to put them in this position and it is not fair to children. But it is not only the theological issue that needs attention. Of greater concern is the way this theology shapes a child's imagination and understanding about prayer.

Catholic children today, like many generations of young Catholics before them, will learn to pray to Mary: "Holy Mary, Mother of God, pray for us sinners now and at the hour of our death." Do we ever stop to ask some basic questions about this prayer and what it expects children (and adults) to imagine: that Mary, in heaven, listens to prayers and spends eternity praying to God for us? What a strange idea of heaven, of eternity and of a God who listens to all these prayers of Mary. Yet, this is the religious imagination into which children are nurtured in the name of good, solid instruction in the Catholic faith.

It is unlikely that Catholic children will stop learning the "Hail Mary" or hearing Mary referred to as "the mother of God." The balance we seek to bring to this situation will come from telling stories about Mary, the girl, young woman, wife, mother, widow and elderly woman. Let us try to make her as human as we possibly can to counteract the unreal theological notions of Mary that have endured over the centuries.

"The Sin of the First Parents"

"Sin came into the world when the first man and woman chose to disobey God."

In order to teach this, teachers must disregard all the available scientific evidence concerning the emergence of the human species. That evidence suggests the first members of the human species would have been incapable of making a moral choice that ruptured connection with God. The issue here is not only about myth versus reality. It also concerns intellectual honesty. It is dishonest to suggest that the first human beings arrived in the world with a fully formed adult conscience, capable of making a moral decision that would affect the future of humanity.

An honest approach would introduce children to the prevailing scientific story of the emergence of the human species and its slow development to moral maturity. That story would also articulate a faith understanding of humanity's connection with an all-pervasive Divine Presence and how awareness of that Presence can affect human behavior. It would explain that sin and evil are uniquely a human phenomenon because while that Presence is always with us, we can refuse to give it expression through our love, care and generosity.

An honest approach would stop telling a story of disconnection from God and replace it with a story that tells of God's constant presence as life unfolded and continues to unfold on this planet. It would be the story of the human species' ongoing struggle to recognize that presence. It would tell also the story of Jesus as someone who tried to enlighten us about the "kingdom of God" – God's presence – in our midst.

"Jesus asked God his Father to send the Holy Spirit to be with us always."

This is theological literalism at its worst. Yet many Christians do not question it, which shows just how deeply and unreflectively we were nurtured into a dualistic religious imagination. We were led to imagine that an

41

elsewhere "Father" aspect of God had to be asked by his "Son" to send the "Holy Spirit" to be with humanity. This traditional Trinitarian scenario requires belief that the Father withheld the "Spirit" aspect of himself until the Son asked him to act.

It would be far better to honor the Hebrew and Christian understanding that the Spirit of God was breathed into all creation – as the very essence and reality of God being always present and sustaining whatever exists. However, that would make God intimately present to everyone. It would overturn the need for a theological schema and Church identity based on the premise that the "Holy Spirit" is "sent", at Jesus' request, only to people who know him and accept him as the unique link with an elsewhere Deity. It would also necessitate a change in the way we understand Jesus as "savior".

"Jesus is our Savior. He has won for us the life of grace."

"Jesus loved us so much that he died for our sins."

We adult educators of children need to be quite clear in our own minds that Jesus is not "savior" because he won access to God's life and love. He did not win that for us. God's loving presence has never been absent from any human being. In order to believe that it was, you have to disregard the notion that living in love and living in God are intrinsically connected. If we disregard that, we are disregarding a basic and foundational claim of the Christian religion. Jesus did not create the connection between living in love and living in God – as if no one who lived before him could have been intimately connected with God in their living and loving. No, he opened people's minds and hearts and eyes to a faith dimension of living and loving they had not grasped: that "God" is here in our everyday living. Jesus is not "savior" because he fixed something or regained access to someone or somewhere. He is "savior" because he set people free from religious ideas and images that locked them into thinking God was not with them. He opened minds and hearts to the always, everywhere present God.

The preceding examples of traditional Catholic belief and religious instruction help to illustrate why prayer has become so problematical for many adult Christians. Consider how we were nurtured into a story of disconnectedness and exile from an elsewhere God and were taught to address prayers to this elsewhere Deity. We learnt that prayer is about speaking to God. Where did we imagine God to be, this God who listens, approves and, if we pray well, responds?

This approach to understanding God and prayer inevitably created irresolvable problems and unanswerable questions for many people: Why did God not grant my prayer? Why did God allow this or that to happen? Or as Pope Benedict once asked, why was God silent during the Holocaust?

How and where did this concept of God as a deity in control of everything arise?

What is somewhat startling for many adult Christians is that it has taken so long for us to even consider the question. We took on board the concept of God given to us through our own Christian educative processes and have largely not stopped to reflect on that understanding as adults.

The Christian notion of God grew out of the worldview of the Hebrew people a thousand years before Jesus. In that worldview earth was the centre of the universe. Against the prevailing belief in many gods, the Hebrew people came to believe in just one all-powerful, all-knowing deity who watched over and controlled everything that happened here. This notion of God gained acceptance with the Hebrew people when they came to believe that God wanted to make a unique covenant with them. Their belief in the covenant and in being God's "chosen people" did wonders for a people struggling to survive political and military upheavals in the region.

Christianity consequently adopted from its mother religion the understanding that:

- God plans and controls and intervenes.

- God has a special love for the poor and the downtrodden.

- God can be offended and punishes accordingly.

- God legislates and demands to be worshipped.

- God listens, notices and reacts to events on earth.

- God has definite opinions on what are essentially cultural matters.

Early Christianity used these ideas about God for its own ends, with one very significant change. It changed focus from the central Jewish idea of a covenant with God to focus on access to God through Jesus. It taught that Jesus connected us once again with this God, that he regained "friendship" with this God, that his life and death "won" this God's forgiveness for our sins, and that only through baptism in the Church Jesus founded could anyone go to the elsewhere place (heaven) where this God lived when they died.

Such notions of God would surely have been news to Jesus, the Jew, who never renounced his Jewish religion and who instructed people to look for and to discover the joy of God close to them in their everyday deeds of being neighbor and living in love. Jesus did not see himself as the connector to an elsewhere God. That understanding – and the words put on Jesus' lips in the Gospels to illustrate it – came from the Christian community in the second half of the first century, especially in the Gospel of John. Far from being the connector or mediator, Jesus was the revealer of God-in-our-midst. That was the "good news" he preached to the lowly and to all who would listen.

The statement we all know so well about living in love and living in God and God living in us, is a wonderful summation of Jesus' message about the Kingdom of God in our midst. But the focus on that wonderful revelation shifted when the young Church community sought to establish its identity by preaching Jesus as the "way" to God and by proclaiming itself as the unique bearer of "salvation", or access to God. The shift in Christian thinking was complete once the theology of original sin took hold, with the belief that everyone is born into a state of separation from God and that only baptism into the Church community could remove the "stain" and restore union with God. The Christian Church conveniently – again for its own ends – overlooked the glaring contradiction between its teaching on "original sin" and Jesus' teaching about God's accessibility to the poor, the downtrodden and whoever lives in love.

Instead of promoting Jesus' vision of God's accessibility

to all people, regardless of religion, institutional Christianity very early shifted the focus to access to an elsewhere God. Jesus and the Church became the "way" to God. The Church's theological and liturgical mindset became fixated on a "fall", on disconnectedness from God, on being exiles, on dependency on an ordained priesthood to bring God's presence to a "fallen race", on exclusive access to God through membership of the Church and its sacraments, and on correct theological thinking.

Despite significant changes in worldview since the time of Jesus, institutional Church leadership has steadfastly refused to examine or modify its notion of God. It continues to do so today. It insists that children learn about God, Jesus and prayer in the context of a worldview unchanged from that in which the Hebrew people shaped their understanding of God three thousand years ago.

If we want generations coming after us to escape this elitist, divisive, narrow-minded, religious mind-set dressed up as "salvation" we need to start at an early age. We can begin by helping children to appreciate that the mystery we call "God" is truly an everywhere reality, accessible to all people, in all places, at all times. We can choose not to tell any stories about God as if God is a Super Being "in heaven". We can do what Jesus did so well: connect everyday living and loving with the mystery we call "God".

The challenge we face in telling biblical stories is to help children avoid literalizing the worldview in which the stories were written. Children need to appreciate how and why the stories developed in biblical times. Children need to understand why people told these stories and how people thought about the world and the universe at that time.

The balance we want to bring in telling our stories is that "God" is an everywhere reality to which everyone has access. We want this to balance the traditional religious stories with their focus on an elsewhere God from whom we were disconnected through Adam's sin.

There are three key elements in this balance. One, telling a contemporary story about who we are and where we came from. Two, speaking about Jesus as someone who opened people's eyes and minds to the Divine Presence in which they lived rather than as someone who re-established connection to an elsewhere deity. Three, telling a story of interconnectedness with everything and everyone *in* God, rather than a story promoting the idea that some people have unique access to or relationship with God by virtue of belonging to a particular religion.

We will start with the contemporary scientific understanding about the universe and our planet's place in it. Some writers refer to this as the "New Story of the Universe". Using this as our foundation we can reflect on God's presence throughout the universe, a presence permeating all that is. We will then be in a position to reflect on Jesus as the revealer of our connectedness with the Divine Presence and then to examine prayer and sacraments and the Church's liturgical year in this framework.

Chapter Three

The Universe Story:
Where We Came From

Most religions use their "creation" stories to articulate their understanding of human relationship with God or gods or the spirit world and to help explain why things are the way they are. Christianity used the Biblical stories of creation to explain death and suffering and to establish that humanity, through Adam's sin, became disconnected from God. Our task today is to use contemporary scientific knowledge about our universe, our planet and the development of life on earth to point to the mystery we call God. This will not be a story about an elsewhere, overseeing God who reacted against a choice made by the first human beings, but the story of an all-pervasive Divine Presence holding everything in relationship. It will not be the story of the "Spirit" of God coming "down" upon a particular group only after Jesus died in order to regain human friendship and connectedness with God, but the story of God's Spirit always present and always active, long, long before Jesus was born. The presence of God, or God's "Spirit" or the Divine Presence (the terms will be used interchangeably in these pages) was not and never can be conditional on what anyone on earth does (not even Jesus). We want to honor what all of us learned early in our Christian upbringing: nothing can exist outside of God; the Divine Presence *is* everywhere, *always*.

Faith educators of future Christian generations would do well to immerse themselves in this "new story" so that it instinctively becomes the foundation on which to stand when speaking to children about God and their relationship with this Mystery. The story highlights the following facts:

- The universe is about 13 billion years old

- It started with a "big bang", a massive explosion. Just before the explosion, everything in our universe – all the galaxies and stars and planets – was contained in a space no bigger than a golf ball. The explosion made everything expand and double in size at an enormous rate. In one million million million million millionths of a second it went from something you could hold in your hand to 10,000,000,000,000,000,000,000,000 bigger!

- After a billion years of expansion and cooling, the first primal stars and galaxies began to form. Eventually, billions of galaxies, each with hundreds of millions of stars took shape as the universe continued to expand. All the hydrogen atoms in water and in our bodies were present in this expansion.

- Eight billion years passed before something very significant happened in the Milky Way Galaxy: a supernova, a giant star, exploded with temperatures of more than 100 million degrees. The explosion manufactured a mass of gas and dust, about 15 billion miles across, containing carbon, nitrogen, iron and other elements. This was the birth of our solar system. Virtually all of the mass, 99.9 percent of it, eventually compressed to make the sun. Other colliding grains of dust formed planets and moons and other smaller objects.

- Every bit of gold and silver and all other precious metals on this planet were manufactured in the intense heat of that explosion. Every carbon atom and every iron atom in our bodies was manufactured then. This means that most of the atoms in our bodies were manufactured in an exploding star and have been on a cosmic journey for billions of years, undergoing transformation after transformation in ways of existing. There are atoms in our bodies, in different format now, that were once a part of dinosaurs. There are atoms in our bodies that were once part of men and women who lived more than a thousand years ago.

- When we die every atom in our bodies will be transformed into another way of continuing on their cosmic journey.

This extraordinary, mind-blowing story has the capacity to change radically our understanding of God, our understanding of ourselves as a life-form, our understanding of how everything and everyone is connected in ways we never suspected, and our understanding of prayer. This is the context in which we must nurture children's religious belief.

The grandeur of this "new story" about our origins evokes awe, wonder and appreciation. It invites us to see ourselves in a wonderful new light: Consider:

- We have our origins in a star! A dying star gave birth to forms of existence (such as life in all its wonderful variations on this planet) far removed from what a star is.

- In the transition from the death of a star to your birth and mine, the universe found a way to come to awareness and reflection and appreciation.

- We give the universe a way to think about itself – and to appreciate itself. Every human person without exception shares this history and reality.

- We also share this history with everything that exists on earth. Everything and everyone is connected in this story.

- For the first time in human history we have a common story to tell about who and what we are. This is a story with the capacity to bond us all together.

- If God is the all-pervasive Mystery holding everything in existence, then for the first time in human history we have a common religious story: everyone and everything is bonded within this Mystery.

- The scientific story tells us that we give the universe a way of coming to awareness. Our religious story tells us that we – all of us in our own unique ways – give God a way of coming to expression in our awareness and our ability to love.

- The universe story draws our attention not only to the stars, but also to the four and a half billion history of this planet. Our awe and appreciation of the gift of a dying star needs to be matched with our awe and reverence and appreciation of this planet which brought us into existence and sustains us. We need to blend our religious story about God and where we encounter God with our appreciation of this wonderful life-giving planet. Since the planet itself is life-giving we are truly walking on sacred ground; this is where we encounter the mystery we call God. Indigenous religions have much to teach us about the Divine Presence in the land and the world around us.

This new universe story directly impacts on the way we speak to children about God and God's presence, about Jesus and about prayer and sacraments.

How does our notion of God and our understanding of the universe and our place in it impact on our understanding of the role of Jesus? On what should we focus when speaking to children about Jesus? How do we lead children in prayer if we want to counterbalance the traditional style of prayer addressed to an elsewhere, listening God? How can we talk to children about sacraments – if sacraments are not to be understood as rituals bringing a Presence from somewhere else? How can we accompany children through the major Christian feasts if we want to avoid the dualism of heaven-earth, up-down imagery and language in which those feasts are presently encased? These issues will be discussed in the following chapters.

Class or home exercise

When articulating Christian faith in the context of the contemporary story about the universe, it may help to use visual presentations. The following suggestions have been useful in helping children and adults to appreciate the universality of the Divine Presence and how that Presence comes to expression on earth.

Materials required: Overhead projector and a pink or red transparency, transparencies of a supernova exploding, the Andromeda galaxy, the planet Venus, and planet Earth. These images are available from the Hubble web site and can be directly printed onto transparencies on most printers. Alternatively, images can be photocopied from books onto transparencies. Transparencies of plants, animals, scenery and people will also be needed.

In a home setting, the pink transparency may be used with images in books and magazines.

Explain that about four and a half billion years ago a supernova, a giant star, in our galaxy exploded. Note that more energy is expended in half an hour of a supernova exploding than the sun uses in millions of years. Project the image and then ask: Where is God? Show the class the pink sheet and explain you want this sheet to represent God's presence. Ask the class where you should place the pink sheet. Comment that many people imagine God is an outside onlooker, with a definite plan in mind. Should the sheet be placed at the top of the picture? Or in just one section of the picture? Hopefully, class members will say that the sheet should be placed over the entire picture. Discuss why this is so: God is the reality holding everything in the picture, holding it altogether, so God has to be everywhere even though we cannot see God. Stress that there is no "outside" of God. Everything happens "in" God.

The key words to use in talking about God in this context are: sustaining; holding everything in existence; holding everything in relationship and connectedness; the source of all power and energy.

If questions such as, "Does God know how things will unfold?" or "Does God know everything?" arise, they would be best handled by asserting that God does not think or know the way we do. It is like asking whether the sun thinks about shining or the wind thinks about what direction to take. God *is*, and everything happens *in* God.

Next, project or show an image of the Andromeda galaxy (which looks much like the Milky Way galaxy). Talk about the number of stars in this galaxy; where the star, our sun, might be in such an image; the distance from one star to another; the speed at which stars are traveling and so on. Earth's place in such a galaxy is like a grain of sand in an area the size of mainland USA. We are never likely to travel outside the realm of this one star we call the "sun". Place the pink transparency over the galaxy to represent God's presence. Use it to demonstrate that God is not "somewhere else"; God holds it all together. Without God being present, nothing would be there.

Show an image of the planet Venus. It is barren; it is hot; it rains sulphuric acid. Some astronomers call Venus "the Hell planet". Place the pink transparency over the image using this to illustrate that the planet is permeated with God's presence. However, because of the conditions of the planet, this is the only way God's presence can come to visibility or be expressed.

Project or show a photo of planet Earth and ask: Where is God? Use the pink overlay again. Look what happens when the conditions are right: God's presence comes to such wonderful expression on this planet.

Highlight the emergence of life *in* and because of God's presence. Show other transparencies of the world around us, again using the pink transparency to illustrate the sustaining presence of God. Use transparencies to illustrate the emergence of human life and its slow development. Use, for example, photos of early art or the early use of tools through to great art and modern technology. God was, and always is, here in these developments. We human beings give God a way of coming to expression! Early human beings did not realize this, however. It took thousands of years for them to come to an understanding of connectedness with God. Some religious groups made the mistake of thinking and teaching that only they were close to God. Some people taught that God could not be close to the sick, the poor and people who struggled.

This is why Jesus is so important to us. He revealed that everyone is connected with God through their living and loving.

The following prayer adapted from *Praying a New Story* could be used as a guide for classroom prayer. Each statement could be read by a different student and all students making the response. The prayer may be further adapted to ensure its language is suitable for a particular class. One way of doing this may be to have class members do their own research on facts about the universe or planet Earth. The teacher could suggest, for example, that someone find out when language began, or art, or the use of tools, or the number of stars in the Milky Way, the number of galaxies, the biggest planet in the solar system and so on, and use the information in the prayer.

Ω: God-with-us

In the star we call the "Sun," converting six hundred million tons of hydrogen into helium every second and doing so for more than four billion years:

We see the presence of the God in whom we believe.

In all the other billions of stars in the Milky Way galaxy and in all their planets:

56

We see the presence of the God in whom we believe.

In the hundreds of billions of other galaxies, each with billions of stars:

We see the presence of the God in whom we believe.

In a universe expanding a billion miles every hour:

We see the presence of the God in whom we believe.

In a planet like Venus, barren and unable to support life as we experience it on earth:

We see the presence of the God in whom we believe.

Here on earth where conditions are ideal for life to appear and prosper:

We see the presence of the God in whom we believe.

In the development of life on earth for hundreds of millions of years:

We see the presence of the God in whom we believe.

In the upheavals on this planet that saw widespread destruction of life and new beginnings, long, long before human life emerged:

We see the presence of the God in whom we believe

In the emergence of human life:

We see the presence of the God in whom we believe.

In the development of language:

We see the presence of the God in whom we believe.

In the use of tools:

We see the presence of the God in whom we believe.

In the development of writing and art:

We see the presence of the God in whom we believe.

In the growth of many and varied cultures:

We see the presence of the God in whom we believe.

In humankind's search for meaning:

We see the presence of the God in whom we believe.

In the great religious leaders:

We see the presence of the God in whom we believe.

In Jesus of Nazareth:

We see the presence of the God in whom we believe.

In you and in me:

We see the presence of the God in whom we believe.

After this shared prayer, lead the children into a quiet prayer time for a few moments and ask them to give thanks silently for the presence of God with them and with one another.

Chapter Four

Jesus: Revealer of God's Presence With Us

Did Jesus understand his task was to win back humanity's access to God? This is a question that adults need to resolve clearly in their own minds because their answer will significantly influence what they tell children and what children will come to understand as Jesus' role. Jesus' preaching about "the kingdom of God" indicates he was intentionally trying to open people's minds to God's presence with them in their everyday living and loving. His preaching indicates he did not think he was bringing that presence to people but that the presence was already there and people were not aware of it. It indicates that Jesus did not operate out of a belief that God was absent or remote from "the crowd" – the struggling lower classes of society. Quite the contrary. His preaching called people into a change of thinking and attitudes, a change necessary for them to break the hold of entrenched thought patterns and images, so that they could believe the "good news" of God-with-them in their daily lives. Surely, Jesus would have been astonished at the Christian notion of a God so remote from humanity that every baby is born into a state of complete separation from that God.

It was only after his death that people began to interpret his role as one of winning access to an elsewhere God. Jesus, the Jew, who preached that being neighbor to one another went hand in hand with intimacy with God, would have been surprised by this thinking and by the theological mind-set that developed as a consequence of this thinking: that he alone had access to God and therefore had to be identified with God in a way no other human person could be. He would have been even more surprised that a Church founded in his name would use this theological development to shape its purpose and identity at the expense of preaching his message that God is accessible to all people, regardless of religious belief, through their loving, visiting, caring, forgiving and being neighbor.

The challenge facing Christians today is to shift discussion from the story so familiar to us – an actual Fall, an elsewhere God who denied access because of Adam's sin, Jesus dying to "save" us and to open the gates of heaven – to another story. This alternative story focuses on God's all-pervasive presence in this vast universe, how the human species gives expression to this Divine Presence and how Jesus allowed this Presence to be visible in all he did as he called people to recognize this Presence in them in their loving.

Jesus shows us how we might connect belief in God's universal presence with contemporary understanding of the universe and our place in it: focus on our human experience and deepen awareness and belief that the Divine Presence is always with us. This is also why we should focus on the human reality that was Jesus of Nazareth – because it is in his very humanness that we see the Divine Presence revealed. If we grasp that, we are better able to grasp and believe that this presence is in and with us in our own humanness. If we fail to focus first on Jesus as human like us we will inevitably make the all too common mistake of theologizing about someone not really like us at all.[5]

When talking with young children, up to about age seven, focus should be on Jesus as a man who lived a long time ago and who wanted people to believe God was close to them. We can say that even though we do not know what God is really like, Jesus told people to think about God the way they would think about a most loving parent. Jesus wanted people to have no fear of God, however they imagined God. And they were not to think that God was a long way from them. We can tell the stories about Jesus' birth, acknowledging God's presence in this child. We can talk about where he lived, how he chose his disciples, how he helped people, who he ate with, the distances he walked, what he told people about God and how God was generous and forgiving. The emphasis here is on presenting Jesus as a human person who did everyday things just as we all do. In this way the foundation is set for children to relate with Jesus as someone who is special, but someone who is also much like them. Later, they will be introduced to other stories that focus on Jesus' ministry, the power and presence of God at work in his actions and his efforts to reveal God's closeness to people.

The Gospel stories in this chapter are intended for use with middle to upper elementary school children because the stories require thinking and reflection skills not yet acquired by younger children. They have been selected because they reveal Jesus in his role of helping the "crowd" discover the wonderful presence of the sacred in their midst: God-with-the-lowly, God with all of us in our living and loving. These particular stories focus

---

5 A fuller treatment of this theme can be found in the author's book, *Is Jesus God? Finding Our Faith* (Crossroad Publishing Co. NY)

attention on Jesus as the revealer of God in our midst rather than on Jesus as the "way" to God. This focus is the counterbalance many religious educators seek as they try to present Jesus in accord with the new universe story and with respect for God's presence at all times in all places and in all people.

If children ask whether Jesus really did do this or that, explain that aspects of some of the stories may have been included later. It may help to outline briefly the development of the gospels:

1. Jesus' own words and actions.

2. A period of forty years after Jesus died during which his followers told stories about him and recounted what he had said. During this time some stories took on a new light or emphasis because of the resurrection. Some stories (for example, stories of his birth) were also added as a way of explaining what people had come to believe about Jesus after he died.

3. People in various communities edited the material into the Gospel format. The final form of each of the Gospels we now have is strongly influenced by the community in which it was edited.

We should keep in mind that the Gospels are not biographies of Jesus. They are faith documents. The stories in the various Gospels were selected by the editors to help people to know and to engage Jesus through the stories. That is also the intent here. Rather than focus on whether an event happened or not, we should focus, and help children focus, on: Why did the early Christian community tell this or that story about Jesus? What insight about him were they trying to convey?

Scriptural scholarship should be used as a guide for determining whether an event "really happened". The story of Jesus walking on water is not included in this chapter but it is a good example of an incident which scriptural scholarship would advise not to accept literally but should be read as a post-Resurrection story against the backdrop of how people of the time viewed the "sea" and where the forces of evil resided and how the followers of Jesus had come to recognize him (after he died) as someone who had overpowered the forces of evil.

Respect for God's universal presence includes belief that God's "power, working in us, can do far more than we can ask or imagine." (Ephesians 3:20) This is an important text to keep in mind whenever questions arise about Jesus performing miracles. Do the miracles prove that he was God? No. They demonstrate that God's power was operative and visible in this man. This was the early Christian understanding and it is clear in the speech placed on Peter's lips at Pentecost:

> "Men of Israel, listen to what I am going to say: Jesus the Nazarene was a man commended to you by God by the miracles and portents and signs that God worked through him when he was among you, as you all know." (Acts 2:22)

We should use the miracle stories to illustrate the presence and the power of God at work in Jesus and in our world, rather than use them to focus on Jesus as someone with unique powers who, therefore, must be essentially different from us. We should present Jesus as someone who believed in this presence and power and acted on that belief.

Another reason for selecting the stories that appear in this chapter is that they can readily be used to lead children into prayer. Suggestions are offered for how this may be done. Generally, two prayer patterns are suggested:

One is the well-known pattern of contemplative Gospel prayer. In this type of prayer we are invited to use our imagination to put ourselves into a Gospel scene. An important aspect of this prayer is to "be there" not merely as an observer, but in order to "meet" Jesus through some interaction. We need to give ourselves quiet time to be with and to reflect on whatever we have imagined in this encounter. We should not be put off by thoughts that this is just "make believe". There is no better way, in fact, to encounter Jesus as friend and life companion than through this type of imaginative prayer.

The second pattern of prayer is more along the lines of traditional meditation in which we engage the story and reflect on what it means for our lives. This pattern may be used to lead children to appreciate what they have in life, to help them reflect on the world in which they live, and above all, to be thankful for God's presence with them.

In presenting these Gospel stories, the author presumes teachers will use educational strategies appropriate to their students. While some suggestions are provided here, it is the teacher's understanding of the children's ages, interests and capabilities that will determine the preferred approach. Similarly, parents and grandparents would modify the language and activities to suit the ability of their child or grandchild. Clearly, some of the stories are more appropriate to older children.

It is important to trust the capacity of children to discuss their reactions, to explore their understanding, to work collaboratively, to express their creativity, to engage in meditation, and to appreciate the spiritual world of wonder, of mystery and of an all-pervasive Divine Presence. These processes are essential if we want to nurture children's faith in a holistic way.

Whatever allowances are required to present the content in the most helpful and relevant manner for children, the over-riding objective of the adult presenting these Gospel stories is twofold: First, to focus on the everywhere reality of the Divine Presence. Second, to focus on Jesus' efforts to help people recognize this Presence within and among them.

Matthew's Gospel

Cure of a leper

(8:1-3. Also in Mk 1:40-45 and Lk 5:12-16)

> After he had come down from the mountain large crowds followed him. A leper now came up and bowed low in front of him. "Sir," he said "if you want to, you can cure me." Jesus stretched out his hand, touched him and said, "Of course I want to! Be cured" And his leprosy left him at once.

Illness was generally considered as a punishment from God for someone's sin. With regard to blindness, for example, people asked Jesus, "Who sinned, this man or his parents that he was born blind?" (Jn 9:2)

At that time people believed contact with a leper would make them "unclean" which meant that God could not be with them.

We should talk with children about how people of the time thought about God – like a father-figure in heaven who looked down on the earth and kept everything under control, who punished people for their sins or sometimes punished their children. This is the cause and effect God: God is responsible for everything that happens because "He" is in control.

This is an opportunity to share with children that we do not hold this view of God even though many people still do. One reason we do not is because it suggests that God is elsewhere, looking down on or over us – and God is not like that at all. God is an everywhere Presence, not a controlling ruler in the heavens.

Jesus wanted to heal the leper, but he wanted to do more than that.

Ask the child or the children: what else might Jesus have wanted to illustrate through this event?

Apart from healing the man, Jesus wanted to show this man and the crowd that God's power and presence was close to them. He wanted to show that the Divine is in unlikely places and people. He wanted to free people from thinking that God could not be with the sick and the poor and the lowly. That is the Good News he brought to the crowd.

Invite children to share any reactions or feelings they had during the story telling. What did they most like about the story? How might the event have changed the person's life? Why did the early followers of Jesus keep telling this story and have it recorded? Explore and discuss the motives and reactions of key people in the story.

The adult presenter should participate and be involved in sharing what he or she liked about the story or why the story is important to him or her. If faith is caught rather than taught then the adult's readiness to share his or her life experience, within reasonable limits, is a vital part of leading children into appreciation of the Gospel stories. As far as possible, adults should draw out insights from the children first before sharing what they think or what the story means to them.

Praying the story

Following discussion, invite the children to enter into silence and stillness.

Ask them to close their eyes and to imagine the story again as you take them through it. The story can be approached from different viewpoints, such as that of the man healed or that of an onlooker. For example:

Imagine you are in the crowd, one of the large number of people following Jesus.

It is a hot day; the road is dusty and you are starting to feel thirsty.

You are about to leave the crowd and go get a drink of water when you notice a leper coming across the street.

He calls out to Jesus, "Sir, if you want to, you can heal me." Everyone stops and looks at Jesus.

They all stop talking and listen. What will Jesus do or say?

Then you see Jesus reach out his hand. He's going to touch the leper!

You hear people in the crowd gasp. He's touching a leper!

He's making himself unclean.

You push forward and hear Jesus say, "Of course I want to.

Be healed!"

And then you see something amazing: the man's skin is healed, made clean, right before your eyes!

You see Jesus and the leper talking quietly to each other.

Jesus embraces him … and then the man rushes off.

Jesus then looks around.

He seems to be looking for someone … and he looks straight at you!

Imagine now he walks over to you, looks into your eyes, calls you by name and says, "John/Mary, know that God is always close to you. Never, never forget that."

Just stay now for a few moments with Jesus saying those words to you.

Cure of the centurion's servant

(8:5-13. Also in Lk 7:1-10)

> When he went into Capernaum a centurion
> came up and pleaded with him. "Sir," he said
> "my servant is lying at home paralyzed, and in
> great pain." "I will come myself and cure him"
> said Jesus. The centurion replied, "Sir, I am not
> worthy to have you under my roof; just give the
> word and my servant will be cured. For I am
> under authority myself, and have soldiers under
> me; and I say to one man: Go, and he goes; to
> another: Come here, and he comes; to my
> servant: Do this, and he does it." When Jesus
> heard this he was astonished and said to those
> following him, "I tell you solemnly, nowhere in
> Israel have I found faith like this. And I tell you
> that many will come from east and west to take
> their places with Abraham, Isaac and Jacob in
> the kingdom of heaven but the subjects of the
> kingdom will be turned out into the dark where
> there will be weeping and grinding of teeth."
> And to the centurion Jesus said, "Go back, then;
> you have believed, so let this be done for you."
> And the servant was cured at that moment.

The common belief was that God certainly could not be
with a Roman soldier since the Romans were viewed as
the enemy.

Jesus was surprised at the man's faith: "Just give the
word and my servant will be cured."

Why would this man have had faith in Jesus?

It could have been because he lived in Capernaum, the town in which Jesus lived. Jesus had moved from Nazareth to live there after his cousin, John, was arrested. (Mt 4:12) It is likely the centurion would have heard stories about Jesus, went to listen and liked what he saw and heard.

Jesus associates this man's faith with the "kingdom of heaven".

What is this "kingdom"? How will people recognize it?

The kingdom of God, the kingdom of heaven, will be seen when people love one another, when people work for peace and justice and fairness, when people share and are generous, when people are ready to forgive the faults of others, when people are aware that God's presence binds them all together. This is why Jesus says "many will come from the east and the west" and will share in God's kingdom. It includes all people.

Once again, there is a miracle, with God's all-pervasive presence working in and through Jesus. But the story is told not only to relate the wonderful healing, but to convey an important message: God's presence can be seen in anyone who loves and cares and acts decently.

Ask the children to talk about people they know or can name who make God's presence visible in the way they live.

Praying the story

The class could be divided into groups and each group reads one of these statements or similar statements composed by the children.

We give thanks for Jesus who cared for people who were sick.

We give thanks for Jesus showing how close God is to everyone.

We give thanks for people we know who make God's kingdom present to us.

We give thanks for all the members of our class and for the friendships we have.

We give thanks for the ways we are kind and helpful to one another.

We pray for our school, that the "kingdom of God" may be seen in the way we work and play together.

We give thanks that God's presence can be seen in people in all religions.

Many cures

(8:16. Also in Mk 1:32-34 and Lk 4:40-41)

> That evening they brought him many who were possessed by devils. He cast out the spirits with a word and cured all who were sick.

"Possessed by devils" could refer to a number of illnesses that can be treated today, but in those days they had no understanding of what caused the illnesses, so people thought they had to be from an evil source. Ask children what illnesses could be included here. For example, epilepsy, stroke, schizophrenia, fever.

Again, the common view was that God could not be with such people. Yet Jesus spent a lot of time with them. He did not believe and did not want people to believe that sickness came from God.

Talk about what it would be like to be cured. What would you think about yourself and God?

Ask children: Where did Jesus get the power to work miracles? Refer again to the Acts of the Apostles text mentioned in the first part of this chapter in which Peter speaks of "the man through whom God did wonderful deeds". God worked through Jesus' care and compassion for people.

In what other ways did God work through Jesus? For example, through his readiness to forgive, his respect for all classes of people, his teaching and his concern for others.

Ask children to name famous people and the way God worked through them. Make a list of names and deeds.

Does God work in you and me? Everyone in this class? Everyone? In what ways does God work in us?

This provides an opportunity to talk about each child having his or her own special gifts, strengths and abilities – the ways God comes to expression in them. Children could share in small groups how they see God working in the other members of the group.

What are the ways God works in your mother, father, brothers and sisters?

Suggest that children make a list for family members – and share this with them at home.

Praying the Story

We give thanks for the way God is present to each one of us.

We give thanks for the ways God works through each one of us.

We want to use our own gifts well so that people will see God working in our lives.

We give thanks for Jesus showing us that God works in everyone who cares and loves.

We give thanks for our family and friends and for everyone who cares and looks after us.

We want everyone, everywhere, to know that all people are close to God.

We will do our best to show God's presence in the way we treat one another.

Cure of a paralytic

(9:1-8. Also in Mk 2:1-12 and Lk 5:17-26)

He got back in the boat, crossed the water and came to his own town. Then some people appeared, bringing him a paralytic stretched out on a bed. Seeing their faith, Jesus said to the paralytic, "Courage, my child, your sins are forgiven." And at this some scribes said to themselves, "This man is blaspheming". Knowing what was in their minds, Jesus said, "Why do you have such wicked thoughts in your hearts? Now, which of these is easier: to say, "Your sins are forgiven", or to say, "Get up and walk"? But to prove to you that the Son of Man has authority on earth to forgive sins – he said to the paralytic – "get up and pick up your bed and go home." And the man got up and went home. A feeling of awe came over the crowd when they saw this, and they praised God for giving such power to men.

People thought the paralytic man's sins caused his illness. God could not be close to him. Jesus, however, saw goodness in the man and his friends. He healed the man.

Ask the children: where is God in this story?

In Jesus? Yes. Who else?

In the paralytic man? Yes. Did he know that? Maybe not. Maybe he knew in his heart he was not a bad person and that is why he trusted that Jesus could heal him.

In the people who carried the man? Surely they were moved by goodness and compassion, but maybe they were not able to see that their goodness and care were ways God acted in and through them.

Is God in and with all the people present? Did they know that? Probably not.

This is a key aspect of these healing stories. The stories are not simply about a holy person with special powers from God. (Note: the crowd praised God "for giving such power to men.")

The cures are Jesus' way of trying to help people understand that God was with them in their everyday lives.

Use the story to name and discuss: who are the men and women today (in the world and also closer to home, in our city or suburb) who show the presence of God in their actions?

How can we act towards one another in ways that show God's presence in what we do?

How can we do this at home, in the classroom or in the playground?

At end of discussion children could be led to share their responses to this question:

When we think about Jesus, and the people we have just discussed and how we want to behave with one another, what do we want to give thanks for?

List what is shared, then lead the children into a time of quiet and stillness. Invite them to close their eyes and to be conscious of breathing in and out.

Be aware of God's presence here with us.

Invite the children to think of one of the items mentioned that they are especially thankful for or invite them to reflect on how each of them shows God's presence in what they do or say.

Praying the Story

We give thanks for the many ways we see God's presence active in the world around us.

We give thanks for Jesus who showed how God is close to everyone and to each of us, no matter who we are.

We give thanks for the people we have mentioned.

We give thanks for each boy and girl here for the ways we show God's presence to one another.

We are thankful that God is within each of us.

We are thankful that we are all close to God.

The call of Matthew

(9:9. Also in Mk 2:13-14 and Lk 5:27-28)

> As Jesus was walking on from there he saw a man named Matthew sitting by the customs house, and he said to him, "Follow me." And he got up and followed him.

In the Gospels of Mark and Luke, the man is named Levi. Luke's Gospel tells us that the man was a tax collector and that "leaving everything" he got up and followed Jesus.

Taxes were imposed both by the Roman occupying forces – "the enemy" – and by the Jewish civil authority. Taxes placed burdens on people. It was inevitable that tax collectors would be greatly disliked. Certainly, it would have been inconceivable to think that God could be with a tax collector. So once again, Jesus turns conventional thinking upside down in his choice of Matthew to be one of his apostles.

What might Jesus have seen in Matthew to choose him?

For example, sincerity, hard work, honesty.

How might Matthew have felt to be chosen?

What lesson can we learn from this?

Think of times we have "judged a book by its cover" and shunned someone.

Are there groups of people who get judged and shunned like this?

Does it happen in our school?

If it does, what can we do about it?

Praying the Story

Lead the class into quiet time, with students closing their eyes, concentrating on their breathing and relaxing.

Imagine now that Jesus comes into this classroom. He looks around and comes to you. Imagine he calls you by your name and says, Terry ... Leonie ... follow me.

Just stay with that thought: you and Jesus together.

What does Jesus see in you that he likes?

Think of one thing in particular that you think Jesus would like about you.

Stay with that thought for a while.

Be thankful for that gift, that quality, that way of acting that Jesus likes about you.

Conclude with:

We give thanks for Jesus who likes each of us;

We give thanks for the gifts each of us has;

We give thanks for people who love us and help us to develop our gifts.

May we use our gifts as best we can.

May we always know that God touches other people's lives through our gifts and our goodness which are expressions of God's presence.

To all this, we say: Amen.

Cure of the woman with a hemorrhage and The official's daughter raised to life

(9:18-26. Also in Mk 5: 21-43 and Lk 8:40-56

While he was speaking to them, up came one of the officials who bowed low in front of him and said, "My daughter has just died, but come and lay your hand on her and her life will be saved". Jesus rose and, with his disciples, followed him.

Then from behind him came a woman who had suffered from a hemorrhage for twelve years, and she touched the fringe of his cloak, for she said to herself, "If I can only touch his cloak, I shall be well again". Jesus turned round and saw her; and he said to her, "Courage, my daughter; your faith has restored you to health". And from that moment the woman was well again.

When Jesus reached the official's house and saw the flute players, with the crowd making a commotion, he said, "Get out of here; the little girl is not dead, she is asleep". And they laughed at him. But when the people had been turned out he went inside and took the little girl by the hand; and she stood up. And the news spread all round the countryside.

What might life have been like for this woman for twelve years?

Why did Jesus invite her to have courage?

Jesus makes it clear that it is her faith that has healed her: "Your faith has restored you to health." She came to Jesus despite the prevailing attitude that people like her were unclean and that she should not touch or approach a man. Her actions took some courage. She touched Jesus because she believed in God's presence in this man.

Would Jesus have believed that he was "holy" and she wasn't? Why or why not?

We need to keep in mind that there is more to these stories than a "holy" man, Jesus, curing someone who was supposedly not "holy". The events are Jesus' way of turning upside down our pre-conceived ideas of where the "holy" is to be found.

Mark's version of these events records that while Jesus was telling the woman her faith had restored her to health, he overheard people from Jairus' house tell Jairus that his daughter had died and that he should not waste Jesus' time in making the journey to his house.

In that account, Jesus urged Jairus to have faith. This is interesting because Jairus was "an official" of the synagogue (refer to Mark and Luke's version). We can presume that Jesus asked this religious leader of the community to have the sort of faith displayed by the woman who had a hemorrhage. Jesus went to the house. He insisted that the people were mistaken and that the girl had not died. He restored her to health (note: not to life).

Invite the children to talk about the effect of Jesus' words and actions on the people involved, especially the woman with the hemorrhage, Jairus, his daughter and family members and friends.

Praying the Story

In a quiet prayer time, invite the children to imagine being in the crowd observing these two events. Take them through each event imaginatively. Finish with a reflection such as:

Imagine Jesus at the end of the day when he moves away to a quiet place to think about the day. He invites you to come with him. Ask him what he is most thankful for from the day's events. What does he tell you?

Imagine he wants to tell you something else.

What does he tell you?

Just sit quietly with that for a few moments.

Conclude with:

Now let us all be thankful for Jesus (pause for some moments after each)

- *for the ways he helped people*

- *for telling people that God is close to them*
- *for telling us that God is always close to us*
- *for being a friend to me*

Cure of two blind men

(9:27-30 and 20:29-34)

> As Jesus went on his way two blind men followed
> him shouting, "Take pity on us, Son of David."
> And when Jesus reached the house the blind
> men came up with him and he said to them, "Do
> you believe I can do this?" They said, "Sir, we
> do." Then he touched their eyes saying, "Your
> faith deserves it, so let this be done for you."
> And their sight returned.

Here is another miracle in which Jesus insists that the Divine works *through personal faith* not through any miraculous powers he might have. God works in their lives. That is the biggest miracle – not that Jesus does it!

These men would have been considered sinners, distant from God, since blindness was understood to be God's punishment for someone's sins. Most people in the crowd would have looked at these men and thought they were worthless. It is highly unlikely that anyone would have considered that the faith of these men could produce such a wonderful result.

Jesus saw things differently.

What enabled him to see what other people could not see?

Perhaps it was his belief that the Divine Presence, God, is in everyone.

Praying the Story

Ask the children to make a list of what the two men would most appreciate seeing after their years of blindness. Arrange for children to share their lists in small groups.

The exercise could also be used to deepen awareness of what we take for granted with our senses of hearing, touch, taste and smell.

Use the list to shape a prayerful litany. Individuals could name an item, for example:

For being able to see beautiful flowers

or

For being able to hear the birds sing in the morning

or

For the smell of my mother's cooking

or

For being able to taste chocolate.

After each statement the class responds:

We give thanks.

Cure of a dumb man

(9: 32-34. Also in Mk 9:14-29)

> They had only just left when a man was brought
> to him, a dumb demoniac. And when the devil
> was cast out, the dumb man spoke and the
> people were amazed. "Nothing like this has ever
> been seen in Israel" they said.

The deaf man and the "boy" in Mark's version of the story
were considered to be "demoniacs" – people in the power
of the "devil".

Mention of the "devil" in this story presents an opportunity
to speak to children about "The Devil" or devils.

Devils were a way of explaining evil. Evil could not come
from God, so people thought there had to be a bad spirit
causing harm and they called this bad spirit the "devil".

Devils were also a way of explaining strange or disturbing
behavior which we now know is caused by illness. It is
most likely that epilepsy was the cause of the dumb man's
disturbing behavior.

If children ask whether devils exist, explain that some
people believe they do, but most people no longer believe
they exist because evil is something people do. People
have to take responsibility for the hurt and the harm
done rather than blaming a devil or someone else.

In Mark's story, the disciples of Jesus were unable to
cure the boy, even though they doubtless wanted to. It
could well be that the disciples were too concerned about
believing *they* could work the miracle, whereas Jesus
was never focused on what he could do, but on what God

could do or what could happen through a person's faith in God.

This is an important aspect to keep in mind. Healing is one gift among many other gifts of the Creative Presence at work in the human species. Prayer and prayer alone will reveal that giftedness to people. And prayer will also reveal to each of us what our true gifts are and how we should use them fruitfully.

In presenting the demoniac stories from both Matthew and Mark, we could explore with children why Jesus could heal and the disciples could not. Clearly Jesus had some gifts or qualities or beliefs the disciples did not have. We could ask the children to name them.

Divide the class into groups of four. Give each child three pieces of paper, one for each of the other members of the group. Ask the children to think about, then write on the piece of paper *Something you do well* or *Something I like about you* for each member of the group. When they have completed the task, ask them to exchange notes. Encourage the children to thank one another for their affirming comments.

Ask the children to consider for whom at home they would like to write a similar note. Maybe they would like to write several notes to take home and distribute.

Praying the Story

Conclude the session with a time of quiet and with words such as:

We give thanks for the sharing here today.

We give thanks for friends who help us.

We give thanks for our own personal gifts and qualities.

We give thanks for all the members of this class.

We give thanks for all the people who love and care for us.

Let us always be ready to help one another. Amen

The distress of the crowds

(9:35-37)

> Jesus made a tour through all the towns and villages, teaching in their synagogues, proclaiming the Good News of the kingdom and curing all kinds of diseases and sickness.
>
> And when he saw the crowds he felt sorry for them because they were harassed and dejected, like sheep without a shepherd.

Why were people harassed and dejected?

(They were heavily taxed, yes, but a greater burden was that their religious leaders did not support or encourage them. Instead these people who were struggling with life heard that they were sinners and that God could not be close to them. That made life doubly hard for them.)

Jesus moved from town to town preaching the "Good News of the kingdom" to these people.

What would Jesus have told these people when he spoke

to them?

Would they have found it easy to believe Jesus?

What do you imagine Jesus would say to us today if he came to this classroom?

Make a collective list of their suggestions.

Is it easy or is it difficult to believe and to do what Jesus wants us to believe and do?

If you were feeling "harassed and dejected", what do you think Jesus might say to you?

Praying the Story

Lead the children into a quiet prayer time.

Use the list complied by the children:

The first thing Jesus would say to us is…

(Name one of the items and pause to give children time to think about it.)

Another thing Jesus would say to us is…

(Work through the list in this way.)

Conclude with:

We give thanks for Jesus and the way he helped people.

We give thanks that he helped them to believe that God loved them and was close to them.

We give thanks for Jesus helping us to know God loves each one of us.

We give thanks for Jesus who guides us and encourages us today.

May we love one another the way Jesus wants us to love. Amen.

The Parable of the Sower

(13:1-9. Also in Mk 4:3-9 and Lk 8:5-8

That same day, Jesus left the house and sat by the lakeside, but such a crowd gathered round him that he got into a boat and sat there. The people all stood on the beach and he told them many things in parables.

He said, "Imagine a sower going out to sow. As he sowed, some seeds fell on the edge of the path, and the birds came and ate them up. Others fell on patches of rock where they found little soil and sprang up straight away, because there was no depth of earth; but as soon as the sun came up they were scorched and, not having any roots, they withered away. Others fell among thorns, and the thorns grew up and choked them. Others fell on rich soil and produced their crop, some a hundredfold, some sixty, some thirty. Listen, anyone who has ears!"

Chapter 13 of Matthew's Gospel has a sense of urgency as Jesus preaches about "the kingdom" or the "kingdom of heaven", both of which refer to the Good News of God's presence with people. The parable of the sower urges people not to waste the benefits of hearing this good news; the parables of the mustard seed and the yeast invite belief that a small group of believers can have a big effect in making God's presence visible; the parables of the treasure and the pearl proclaim Jesus' belief that nothing is more important than establishing or making visible God's presence through the way we love.

Jesus preached good news about God with people. Some people heard the news with great joy, but it was like seed falling on rock – they would quickly forget the good news as soon as some hardship came along. Others who heard the good news would neglect its message by chasing riches or would later forget because they were busy about many things.

How can we make sure this will not happen with us?

How can we be like the seed that falls on rich soil and yields a good harvest?

If we hear what Jesus says and believe it, what difference would this make to our lives?

Praying the Story

Have the children draw or paint their impressions of the Parable of the Sower. Where would they put themselves in the drawing?

When they have finished and have had an opportunity to talk about their drawing or painting, ask them to write a short prayer to accompany it.

Mustard seed and Yeast

(13:31-33. Also in Mk 4:30-32 and Lk 13:18-19)

> He put another parable before them "The kingdom of heaven is like a mustard seed which

a man took and sowed in his field. It is the smallest of all the seeds, but when it has grown it is the biggest shrub of all and becomes a tree so that the birds of the air come and shelter in its branches."

He told them another parable. "The kingdom of heaven is like the yeast a woman took and mixed in with three measures of flour till it was leavened all through."

What is Jesus wanting to tell us through these parables?

(If just a few good people really believe, then great things can happen.)

Tell stories how one person mobilized change or activity e.g. Martin Luther King, Mahatma Gandhi, Joan of Arc, Nelson Mandela.

Who gives leadership like this today? Who are our heroes? Why? How do they make "the kingdom of heaven" visible here on earth?

What would the "kingdom of heaven" (here on earth!!) look like? How could people work together so that we could see it? For example, through fairness, justice, sharing, respect for all, generosity.

Praying the Story

Shape a litany prayer using the men and women mentioned and their contributions.

For example, one class member says:

"We give thanks for Nelson Mandela."

And the class or one member of the class responds:

"We give thanks for the way he forgave people and the way he united people in peace."

Mark's Gospel

Cure of man with a withered hand

(3:1-6. Also in Mt 12:9-14 and Lk 6:6-11)

> He went again into a synagogue, and there was a man there who had a withered hand. And they were watching him to see if he would cure him on the Sabbath day, hoping for something to use against him. He said to the man with the withered hand, "Stand up out in the middle!" Then he said to them, "Is it against the law on the Sabbath day to do good, or to do evil; to save life, or to kill?" But they said nothing. Then, grieved to find them so obstinate, he looked angrily round at them, and said to the man, "Stretch out your hand". He stretched it out and his hand was better. The Pharisees went out and at once began to plot with the Herodians against him, discussing how to destroy him.

The Sabbath was a day when no work was to be done, so some people were watching Jesus to see if he would break the law. He tested them by asking: is it more important to keep a law than to do good? If you need to break a law to save a life, should you do so?

Invite class discussion: Why do we have laws and rules? Highlight that laws are for the good of a family or a school or a society.

Why were people "watching" Jesus?

Jesus looked "angrily" at them. What do you imagine would make Jesus angry?

It could be any number of issues, such as neglect of the sick and the poor; seeking riches and wealth while hurting people; placing more importance on rules rather than on caring for people.

What might the man do afterwards?

He would surely want to show off his cured hand, work with it, and spread the news about Jesus.

Praying the Story

Lead the children into a time of silent reflection.

Imagine you are the person with a withered hand. Imagine what this hand is like: the fingers are very small and out of shape. You cannot move them at all. You have not been able to use this hand for some time. Now imagine Jesus comes and stands in front of you. He looks at you kindly. Just stay imagining that for a few moments. Jesus is very friendly with you. Imagine he smiles at you – and you smile back at him. He reaches out, takes your hand and holds it firmly while you are looking at him. You then look at your hand – and your hand has become normal!

Now imagine what you would do after this. Take a few minutes with this, and if you get distracted, come back to thinking about what happened afterwards.

Invite the children to share what they imagined.

Conclude with a prayer such as the following:

We give thanks for the kindness of Jesus.

We give thanks for the ways he helped people and for the times he healed people.

We give thanks for his friendship with each of us.

We give thanks for our health,

for our eyes and our ears

and our hands and our feet.

For all the good things we have in life, we give thanks.

Amen.

Jesus with children

(9:33-37 and 10:13-16. Also in Lk 18:15-17)

They came to Capernaum, and when he was in the house he asked them, "What were you arguing about on the road?" They said nothing because they had been arguing which of them was the greatest. So he sat down, called the Twelve to him and said, "If anyone wants to be first, he must make himself last of all and servant of all. He then took a little child, set him in front of them, put his arms round him, and said to them, "Anyone who welcomes one of these little children in my name, welcomes me; and anyone who welcomes me welcomes not me but the one who sent me." (9:33-37)

People were bringing little children to him for him to touch them. The disciples turned them away, but when Jesus saw this he was indignant and said to them, "Let the little children come to me; do not stop them; for it is to such as these that the kingdom of God belongs. I tell you solemnly, anyone who does not welcome the kingdom of God like a little child will never enter it." Then he put his arms round them, laid his hands on them and gave them his blessing. (10:13-16)

Jesus used these two encounters with children to teach his disciples about service. In the first incident (chapter 9), the apostles had argued about who was the greatest among them. This must have been very disappointing for Jesus! It indicated that they had totally misunderstood what he was trying to accomplish. He was not interested in power or control or authority. He wanted to see "the kingdom of God" made visible by the way people cared for one another. Service to others is essential for this to be accomplished. In both scenes, the apostles and the disciples of Jesus seem caught up in their own importance, to the point of rebuking people for bringing children for Jesus to touch. In their minds Jesus had far more important things to do than to be bothered with children. This is hardly a frame of mind open to service of others. Embracing the children demonstrates Jesus' openness and service to others. But it does more: his actions challenge all Christians to a particular kind of openness if the presence of God is to be seen in what they do and say. It is the openness that children display in their trust, in their unfiltered acceptance of goodness and generosity, in their delight of the here and now, and in their capacity to live with wonder and mystery. In these two encounters, Jesus challenged the apostles to be open and trusting like the children rather than secretly discussing their own importance. He also wanted them to learn that if they were to be leaders they had to be of service to others; they must be ready to help people and let them know they cared for them.

Talk about ways this is done at school, in the family; and in society.

Praying the Story

Lead the children into a quiet time in which they imagine they are the child that Jesus embraced. Ask them to imagine the gentleness of his arms around them. Give them time to reflect on what Jesus might say to them.

After the reflection, invite the children to write a short prayer that captures their time spent with Jesus.

Cure of a blind man

(10:46-52)

> They reached Jericho; and as he left Jericho with his disciples and a large crowd, Bartimaeus (that is, the son of Timaeus) a blind beggar, was sitting at the side of the road. When he heard that it was Jesus of Nazareth, he began to shout and say, "Son of David, Jesus, have pity on me". And many of them scolded him and told him to

keep quiet, but he only shouted all the louder, "Son of David, have pity on me". Jesus stopped and said, "Call him here". So they called the blind man. "Courage," they said "get up; he is calling you." So throwing off his cloak, he jumped up and went to Jesus. Then Jesus spoke, "What do you want me to do for you?" "Rabbuni," the blind man said to him, "Master, let me see again." Jesus said to him, "Go; your faith has saved you". And immediately his sight returned and he followed him along the road.

With most miracles we do not know the names of people cured. Here the man is named: Bartimaeus. Why this man's name is recorded when the names of most other people cured are not? Possibly because, at the end of the story, "he followed Jesus along the road". Perhaps he became a follower and was known to the community whereas many others may have drifted away after they were healed.

This man had not always been blind: "Let me see again" he asked Jesus.

What do you think he most missed seeing when he went blind? What would you most miss?

Bartimaeus was urged by his friends to have courage. We too need courage at different times. Can you think of such occasions in your life?

Can you think of a time when a friend or a family member needed to have courage?

Think of some other people who showed great courage in what they did.

Can you think of times when Jesus himself needed to have courage?

Praying the Story

We know Jesus understood the need for courage.

May he be a friend we turn to when we need to have courage.

May we be a good support when a friend needs help.

May we find the courage to stand up for what is right and good

We give thanks for people who show us how to have courage.

We give thanks for the power of God's presence always with us, always leading us to be strong and courageous in doing what is right.

Amen.

Luke's Gospel

Call of Peter

(5:1-11)

> Now he was standing one day by the Lake of Gennesaret, with the crowd pressing round him listening to the word of God, when he caught sight

of two boats close to the bank. The fishermen had gone out of them and were washing their nets. He got into one of the boats – it was Simon's – and asked him to put out a little from the shore. Then he sat down and taught the crowds from the boat.

When he had finished speaking he said to Simon, "put out into deep water and pay out your nets for a catch. "Master," Simon replied, "we worked hard all night long and caught nothing, but if you say so, I will pay out the nets". And when they had done this they netted such a huge number of fish that their nets began to tear, so they signalled to their companions in the other boat to come and help them; when these came, they filled the two boats to sinking point.

When Simon Peter saw this he fell at the knees of Jesus saying, "Leave me, Lord; I am a sinful man". For he and all his companions were completely overcome by the catch they had made, so also were James and John, sons of Zebedee, who were Simon's partners. But Jesus said to Simon, "Do not be afraid; from now on it is men you will catch". Then bringing their boats back to land, they left everything and followed him.

Fishermen were not thought of very highly. People believed that God could not be close to them. They believed this because they had heard it all their lives from their religious leaders. So Peter really thought that a holy man like Jesus should not and would not be friendly with him – or help him catch fish! It is interesting that Jesus tells

Peter not to be afraid. Why might Peter have been afraid, since as a fisherman he would not have been lacking in physical strength?

Once again Jesus was trying to overturn people's idea of God. He was effectively saying the belief that people like Peter could not be close to God was wrong.

Some religious leaders would not have been happy with Jesus' message. They liked to enforce the laws and the customs of the day and to keep people in their place.

Why did Jesus choose Peter?

How do you imagine Peter felt after this event?

What might he have talked about that night with his friends?

What might he have thought and felt about Jesus?

Praying the Story

Lead the children into a quiet time of reflection on the Gospel story. Adapt the scene to make it inclusive for girls. Peter and his wife are standing by his boat and Jesus comes and speaks to both of them. He wants Peter to be an apostle. What might his wife think about this? What does she say to Jesus? What does Jesus say to her? Imagine Peter speaking with his wife about what happened. What was it like for him to be accepted by Jesus? What was it like for her to know this holy man accepted and respected her husband?

The class could work together to create a dramatic presentation of what emerged from their reflection.

Eating with sinners

(5:29-32. Also in Mt 9:10-13 and Mk 2:15-17)

> In his honour Levi held a great reception in his house, and with them at table was a large gathering of tax collectors and others. The Pharisees and their scribes complained to his disciples and said, "Why do you eat with tax collectors and sinners?" Jesus said to them in reply, "It is not those who are well who need the doctor, but the sick."

Luke's version of this event makes clear that Levi/ Matthew hosted this meal. He must have been a wealthy person to hold a "great reception" with many guests. He obviously gave up a great deal to follow Jesus.

The question from the Pharisees and scribes indicates their belief that if Jesus mixed and ate with sinners they would lead him astray. A holy man should not mix in such company.

Ask children who the "sinners" might be?

Why did Jesus meet with them and eat with them?

What is special about eating a meal with people? What does it show?

What do you imagine Jesus might have been talking about with them?

Emphasize Jesus assuring them that the Divine was with them. They would be surprised to hear this from a holy man. If they asked him, "How would we know this is true? How would we recognize the Divine Presence in our lives?" Jesus would have told them: when you care, when you visit, when you look after one another, when you are generous and helpful to one another.

Praying the Story

Lead the class into quiet time, with students closing their eyes, concentrating on their breathing and relaxing.

Imagine you are a tax collector and people do not like you.

Matthew, your friend, another tax collector, meets you and tells you he is leaving his work to follow Jesus. He invites you to come to his house that night for a big party.

You go to the large house and many people are there.

Imagine yourself moving around and having a good time ... or maybe you sit quietly in a corner.

Jesus then comes and stands or sits with you. He is very kind and gentle... He seems to like you.

What do you imagine he says to you?

What do you say to him?

The woman who was a sinner

(7:36-50)

One of the Pharisees invited him to a meal. When he arrived at the Pharisee's house and took his

place at table, a woman came in, who had a bad
name in the town. She had heard he was dining
with the Pharisee and had brought with her an
alabaster jar of ointment. She waited behind
him at his feet, weeping, and her tears fell on
his feet, and she wiped them away with her
hair; then she covered his feet with kisses and
anointed them with the ointment.

When the Pharisee who had invited him saw
this, he said to himself, "If this man were a
prophet, he would know who this woman is that
is touching him and what a bad name she has.
Then Jesus took him up and said, "Simon, I have
something to say to you". "Speak, Master" was
the reply. "There was once a creditor who had
two men in his debt; one owed him five hundred
denarii, the other fifty. They were unable to pay,
so he pardoned them both. Which of them will
love him more?" "The one who was pardoned
more, I suppose," answered Simon. Jesus said,
"You are right".

Then he turned to the woman. "Simon," he said"
you see this woman? I came into your house,
and you poured no water over my feet, but she
has poured out her tears over my feet and wiped
them away with her hair. You gave me no kiss,
but she has been covering my feet with kisses
ever since I came in. You did not anoint my
head with oil, but she has anointed my feet with
ointment. For this reason I tell you that her
sins, her many sins, must have been forgiven
her, or she would not have shown such great
love. It is the man who is forgiven little who

shows little love". Then he said to her, "Your sins are forgiven". Those who were with him at table began to say to themselves, "Who is this man, that he even forgives sins?" But he said to the woman, "Your faith has saved you; go in peace."

There was a usual form of welcome, mentioned in the story, which was not given to Jesus. Why would Simon have chosen not to welcome Jesus properly?

Why did the woman come to the house?

Discuss the bravery of the woman for daring to enter the house.

Her attitude to herself had obviously undergone dramatic change. The story makes it clear she had already experienced forgiveness before this meeting and this is what led her to "show such great love" and to act courageously, tenderly and graciously. Most likely she had experienced through Jesus' teaching, hope for people like herself and wanted to thank him for what he was preaching. He gave people like her dignity. She had learnt that the presence of God was with her and she acted according to that presence. Her belief in that presence "has saved her".

Praying the Story

Lead the children into imaginative Gospel prayer: Be the woman coming up the pathway to the house. (Do not presume boys are incapable of imagining this scene.) What is she feeling? Why does she want to meet Jesus?

What it is like for her when she enters the house? What does she sense about Jesus as she approaches him? She washes and dries Jesus' feet. Why is she crying? These are not tears of sorrow; they are tears of joy because Jesus accepts her and does not turn away from her. She feels, she knows he forgives her even though she is known as a "sinner". Dwell on her sense of being forgiven and accepted. If this were you, rather than the woman, what do you imagine Jesus would say to you today?

Good Samaritan

(10:29-37)

A man was once on his way down from Jerusalem to Jericho and fell into the hands of brigands; they took all he had, beat him, and then made off, leaving him half dead. Now a priest happened to be travelling down the same road, but when he saw the man, he passed by on the other side. In the same way a Levite who came to the place saw him and passed by on the other side. But a Samaritan traveller who came upon him was moved with compassion when he saw him. He went up and bandaged his wounds, pouring oil and wine on them. He then lifted him on to his own mount, carried him to the inn and looked after him. Next day he took out two denarii and handed them to the innkeeper; "Look after him," he said "and on my way back I will make good any extra expense you have." "Which of these three, do you think, proved himself a neighbour to the man who fell into the brigands' hands?" "The one who took pity on him," he replied. Jesus said to him, "Go, and do the same yourself".

The background to this story (10:25-28) is a lawyer wanting to know what is really important in life. Jesus says: love God and your neighbor. The man wants to know who is his neighbor. Jesus says it is not a matter of *who* our neighbor is but a matter of *being* neighbor, even to the most unlikely (and unliked!) people. Jesus shows *how* to be neighbor.

Locate Samaria on a map – between Galilee to the north and Judea to the south. The Samaritans considered themselves Jews but were shunned by other Jews because they had inter-married with Assyrian conquerors of the land centuries before. After their return from the Exile five hundred years before Jesus, the Jewish people, focusing on their identity as God's Chosen People, adopted a policy of exclusion towards Samaritans and "Gentiles" in order to be faithful to their Covenant with God.

So Jesus knew he was upsetting strong religious and cultural boundaries when he made a Samaritan the key character in his story. His story was meant to shock, to disturb and to make people question long-cherished assumptions and prejudices.

Jesus' lesson is that where you see care and concern, you see the presence of God. God's presence is not limited to any one religious group. It transcends all religious boundaries.

Children should be helped to see how this story applies to people of other religious faiths, to people with no religious affiliation and to people whose ethnic and cultural background differs from their own. Who or what groups come to mind? Are there some attitudes we have towards people who are different from ourselves that we should change?

This would be an ideal setting in which to lead children to an appreciation of "The Golden Rule" across the world's religions and even among people with no religious affiliation: do unto others as you would like done to you; be neighbor as you would like people to be friendly and helpful to you. To see the Rule articulated so clearly in so many places gives hope that religion bears the potential to bring people together in common concern and need not be divisive or threatening. Here are some examples: [6]

Confucianism:

One word which sums up the basis of all good conduct: *loving-kindness*. Do not do to others what you do not want done to yourself. (Confucius. Analects 15.23)

Hinduism:

This is the sum of duty: not do to others what would cause pain if done to you. (Mahabharata 5:1517)

Islam:

Not one of you truly believes until you wish for others what you wish for yourself. (Muhammad. 13th of the 40 Hadiths of Nawawi)

Judaism:

What is hateful to you, do not do to your neighbor. This is the whole *Torah*; all the rest is commentary. Go and

6   The Golden Rule Poster produced by Paul McKenna and Scarboro Missions, a Canadian Catholic Missionary Community. Scarborough, On M1M 1M4

learn it. (Hillel. Talmud, Shabbath 31a)

Taoism:

> Regard your neighbor's gain as your own gain and your neighbor's loss as your own loss. Lao T'zu. T'ai Shang Kan Ying P'ien 213-218)

Sikhism:

> I am a stranger to no one; and no one is a stranger to me. Indeed, I am a friend to All. (Guru Granth Sahib, pg 1299)

Baha'i Faith:

> Lay not on any soul a load that you would not wish to be laid on you, and desire not for anyone the things you would not desire for yourself. (Baha'u'llah, Gleanings)

Native Spirituality:

> We are as much alive as we keep the earth alive. (Chief Dan George)

It would be beneficial also to introduce children to the Parliament of the World's Religions, an organization committed to respecting "life and dignity, individuality and diversity, so that every person is treated humanely, without exception". The Parliament is a beacon of hope for a world suspicious and dismissive of religion that is locked into elitism, fanaticism, dogmatism and authoritarianism.

Praying the Story

We give thanks for God's presence in all people, at all times.

We give thanks for different religions and how they all encourage people to love one another.

We give thanks for people of every color, race and ethnic group and the way they all give expression to God's presence in our world.

We give thanks for the way God's Spirit has always been active in human culture and history.

We give thanks for different customs, for the ways people dress differently, for the ways people think differently, and for how God's Spirit is expressed in these differences.

We know that the same Spirit of God active in all places is present and active in our lives.

May we always show this Spirit of God in the ways we accept and act towards other people.

And may we respect people we think are different from us, especially in their language, customs and religious beliefs.

Amen.

Parables of God's mercy:

The lost sheep; the lost drachma; the lost son

(15:1-32)

The introduction is the key to these parables: "The tax collectors and the sinners" were seeking Jesus' company to hear what he had to say. He clearly "welcomed and ate with" them.

The religious leaders complained: They are sinners! He should not mix with them! A holy person would not do this!

So Jesus challenged the leaders to turn their thinking upside down. God's presence *can* be encountered among these people. And God would "welcome" them. God would be "at home" with such people. The very idea was scandalous to righteous people who believed that only strict adherence to religious laws could find favor with God. Jesus attempted to expand their notion of God. God's generosity and acceptance and willingness to forgive far exceeds anything these people could imagine or be comfortable with.

The parables in this section are definitely not just "nice" stories about God. They are stories intended to shock people and to disturb entrenched notions about religious and social behavior. If Jesus' understanding of God was right then much would have to change!

The audience listening to the parable about the lost sheep would have been acutely aware that no shepherd would ever leave ninety nine sheep to go looking for a stray sheep. That would expose the ninety nine to great risk. The message is clear: God's activity is not measurable by human wisdom and human safeguards. God has unimaginable care and love for the "lost".

How must the "lost" people in the crowd have rejoiced when they heard this parable!

How must the men questioning Jesus have squirmed. And how must they have deepened their opinion that this man's views were dangerous to the good order of society.

The theme of God (or "heaven" or "the angels of God") rejoicing over a repentant sinner continues in the parable of the woman rejoicing over her lost coin. Jesus' intent is clear: he wants people in the crowd to know that the goodness in their hearts finds great delight and acceptance with their God.

In the parable of the "lost Son" or the "loving father" Jesus teaches that his God is not someone who keeps a record of wrongs.

This parable can also be used to talk about death. Some people are fearful of "meeting God" when they die. Jesus has given us a wonderful image: death is like the embrace the lost son receives when he returns to his father. There is no judgment, no condemnation, only love and an embrace beyond imagining. That is what death will be like for us. There is nothing to be feared on the other side of death. The parable is the best counterbalance we have to widespread notions of a God who does not unreservedly embrace good people in death, a God who sends people to some other place (Purgatory) where they need to be thoroughly cleansed before God could possibly welcome them.

We should keep in mind and remind children that all of our language and all of our images about what happens after people die cannot describe the reality. Death will not be like meeting a Personal God who will literally embrace us. The image of a Personal God embracing us is only an image to help us believe in something wonderful and beyond our imagining when we are transformed into another way of living on in God.

Praying the Story

Invite the children to write a prayer with the theme:

I *give thanks to Jesus because he teaches me …*

For example,

I give thanks to Jesus because he teaches me that God is always ready to forgive me.

I give thanks to Jesus because he teaches that God is like a most loving father or mother.

I give thanks to Jesus because he teaches me that I should rejoice in God's love for me.

Invite the class to share their prayers.

Ten lepers

(17:11-19)

Now on the way to Jerusalem he travelled along the border between Samaria and Galilee. As he entered one of the villages, ten lepers came to meet him. They stood some way off and called to him, "Jesus! Master! Take pity on us." When he saw them he said, "Go and show yourselves to the priests". Now as they were going away they were cleansed. Finding himself cured, one of them turned back praising God at the top of his voice and threw himself at the feet of Jesus and thanked him. The man was a Samaritan. This made Jesus say, "Were not all ten made clean? The other nine, where are they? It seems that no one has come back to praise God, except this foreigner." And he said to the man, "Stand up and go on your way. Your faith has saved you."

This story should be linked with the parable of the Good

Samaritan. The one who came back was a Samaritan.

Why did the followers of Jesus keep this story alive and keep telling it? It would be a good question to put to children.

The story highlights what is central to Jesus' belief and ministry – the non-religious, the unacceptable person, the one supposedly distant from God and outside the circle of God's favor, acts decently. God's loving presence is there.

Why didn't the other nine give thanks? It was not just that they forgot or were too selfish. There is something deeper at stake: these men were not attuned to God's presence within them. If they had been, they could not have failed to act graciously – which includes appreciation of goodness, gratitude and service to others. In other words, if we reflect on and believe that God-is-with-us in all we do, we will act more lovingly and graciously.

Praying the Story

Discuss the story from the viewpoint of the man who came back and thanked Jesus. What was life like before he met Jesus? What was the reaction of friends and relatives when he met them and showed what had happened? How did life change for him? For what would he be most thankful?

What is the story asking of us?

Are there things we take for granted and never think to give thanks for?

Make a list.

Conclude with a prayer in which children mention the

113

items listed and then respond, for example,

For our mothers who cook for us every day: All: *We give thanks.*

For our bus drivers: All: *We give thanks*

Zacchaeus

(19:1-10)

He entered Jericho and was going through the town when a man whose name was Zacchaeus made his appearance; he was one of the senior tax collectors and a wealthy man. He was anxious to see what kind of man Jesus was, but he was too short and could not see him for the crowd, so he ran ahead and climbed a sycamore tree to catch a glimpse of Jesus who was to pass that way. When Jesus reached the spot he looked up and spoke to him, "Zacchaeus, come down. Hurry, because I must stay at your house today." And he hurried down and welcomed him joyfully. They all complained when they saw what was happening. "He has gone to stay at a sinner's house" they said. But Zacchaeus stood his ground and said to the Lord, "Look, sir, I am going to give half my property to the poor, and if I have cheated anybody I will pay him back four times the amount". And Jesus said to him, "Today salvation has come to this house, because this man too is a son of Abraham, for the Son of Man has come to seek out and save what was lost."

Zacchaeus was an important man in the community. He was an honorable man, but because he was a tax collector he was considered to be a "sinner". God could not be close to such a man. Jesus knew people believed this. He also knew that if he associated with Zacchaeus many people would think he lowered himself by mixing with a sinner and would criticise him.

Jesus caused a scandal by going to the home of Zacchaeus. He clearly believed that generosity and service were to be found among the sinners and outcasts of society. However, there is more to the story than just noticing that Zacchaeus is a good man at heart. Jesus wanted people to recognize their goodness and generosity as evidence of God's presence working in their lives. These people are not "sinners", distant from God at all. This was the Good News Jesus preached.

Praying the Story

Lead children reflectively through the story from the viewpoint of Zacchaeus. Imagine his efforts to catch a glimpse of Jesus. Running alongside the crowd he was not able to see clearly. He climbed a tree. What must he, a well-known person in town, have felt like, up a tree? What did he feel when Jesus first stopped and looked at him? Embarrassed? What did Jesus say to him? How did that change the way Zacchaeus felt? What did he think and feel as he rushed home? How did he welcome Jesus in his house?

Afterwards, discuss with children what this story means for us today.

Widow's mite

(21:1-4)

As he looked up he saw rich people putting their offerings into the treasury; then he happened to notice a poverty-stricken widow putting in two small coins, and he said, "I tell you truly, this poor widow has put in more than any of them; for these have contributed money they had over, but she, from the little she had has put in all she had to live on."

Jesus wanted people to see that wherever generosity was shown, there was evidence of the "kingdom" or the presence of God, God's Spirit working in and through people. He wanted people to recognize this – whatever their state in life.

This woman was truly generous. The rich people made a show of being generous but what they gave cost them little. But she gave "from the little she had".

Where do we find such generosity today?

Tell a story you know about someone being generous.

What would Jesus think of these people?

When were you last generous to someone?

When was someone generous to you?

Maybe there are people who are generous to us and we do not realize it. Can you think of such instances?

Praying the Story

In a silent period, invite children to call to mind people who have been and who are generous to them.

What am I most thankful for? To whom am I most thankful?

How can I show my appreciation?

Conclude with a prayer such as:

We give thanks for people who are kind and generous to us:

We believe the Spirit of God is expressed in their goodness.

We give thanks for all the good things we have in life.

We give thanks for the Spirit of God always with us.

May we be always truly thankful for what we have,

and may we always be ready to share the good we have with others

so that God's Spirit will shine in our lives.

Amen.

Chapter Five

Prayer: Deepening Awareness
of the Divine Presence

God, the Divine Presence, the Spirit of Life and Love – whatever names we use for this Mystery permeating and holding all things in existence – comes to visibility in the human reality we are. Prayer for all of us, adults and children, is the means we have to deepen awareness of this wonderful privilege. It is the means to deepen awareness that every human person shares the same privilege, regardless of race and religion. It is the means to deepen awareness that we are intimately connected and bonded with our planet, our universe and all that is *in* this Presence. It is the means to accept our responsibility for making the Presence of God visible and effective in the human species. Prayer is a way to express our commitment to give the best possible expression we can to this sacred presence. Prayer has to both encourage and challenge us: we pray to be better than we are.

Prayer is not about words addressed to an elsewhere God. Prayer is about reflection on life and the interconnectedness of everyone and all things within God's Presence. Prayer is an affirmation of this presence and of our dignity. Through prayer we express gratitude for life and for all that is good and beautiful in our lives. Our gratitude is not addressed to a listening deity. It has more to do with standing and facing life in a spirit of appreciation and gratitude and allowing this spirit of appreciation to shape who we are and what we do.

Prayer should also express our longings, joys, and fears. It should help us do what the great spiritual leaders throughout the ages assert is necessary for a worthwhile spiritual life: to be in touch with our inner selves. This cannot be done without periods of silence and reflection.

When praying with children, we should consciously strive to avoid any talk about prayer or saying prayers that suggest:

- God is somewhere else

- God is like a big daddy in the sky

- God controls everything

- God listens, like a human person.

Prayer should steep children in the conviction that everything in the universe is inter-related and that the Divine permeates all that is. This theme needs to be taken up again and again and affirmed frequently as students study and learn about the world in which they live. Prayer should lead us beyond our own personal concerns to contemplation of the Divine Presence everywhere and to the challenges such contemplation will inevitably raise. It will lead us to reflect on respect for other people, how we protect the environment, our concern for economic and political injustice, our involvement in breaking down social and ethnic barriers, and our willingness to take action against the materialism and selfishness to which young minds are exposed.

Jesus and Prayer

The heart of Jesus' preaching to people was his ability to name everyday human activity as the arena of the Divine – a concept that most of his listeners found not only strange but difficult to accept. He was brilliant, really. And so simple! Look at, reflect on your everyday activity, your visiting, being neighbor, feeding the family, sharing food – and start saying to yourself and convince yourself that this is what gives expression to the Divine Presence. Your loving and caring and generosity are indicators that this Presence is active in your life. So keep *doing* it, and make the "reign" of God visible in your families and in society. *Be neighbor* to all. That was Jesus' dream.

This is perhaps the greatest insight we can have about ourselves from contemplating the message of Jesus: we give human expression to whatever God is. Undoubtedly, Jesus would want children to learn from his insights. Here, then, is the key we are looking for in helping children to pray: keep naming and affirming everyday experiences of good behavior as the Divine coming to wonderful expression in their lives. Keep telling children this good news and keep reminding them how privileged we all are to know this. Keep challenging them to show this Presence in all they do and say. What a solid grounding for a wholesome spirituality to take into their teenage years and beyond!

We can connect prayer with personal experience by encouraging children to talk about their daily lives. For example, what has happened, whom they have met, what did it feel like, what are they thankful for, and so on. The prayerful aspect lies in leading children to an awareness that the Spirit of God is present with and active in them in their everyday activities.

Meditation

Many schools are discovering that daily classroom meditation programs are proving to be wonderfully beneficial. At a basic level they provide a counterbalance to competitiveness, to noise, to activity, and to engagement with technology, especially computers, television and mobile phones. In the silence, children can be led to relax and to be in touch with a sacred inner space and the sense that the sacred permeates everything and everyone. This sense of the sacred everywhere is readily grasped and appreciated by children. It would doubtless stay with them if adults nurtured it properly and protected children from formalized religion's fixation on an elsewhere God.

Meditation in the classroom is not a lengthy, difficult exercise. All it needs is five minutes, preferably every day at the same time, when students are led into stillness and quietness, usually through sitting comfortably, closing their eyes, being attentive to their breathing and to slowing down their bodies and their minds. That may take one or two minutes. The teacher then announces or rings a small bell to indicate that the meditation time has begun. The children will need to be prepared beforehand to choose something they will "sit with" in this quiet period. It could be a mantra which they are encouraged to repeat over and over to themselves, coming back to it whenever their thoughts are distracted. It could be a simple thought, such as "God lives in me", or a line adapted from a story about Jesus, imagining Jesus saying

"Of course I want to help you." Or maybe a child will just want to reflect on an act of kindness with the thought, "Here, I experienced God in my life."

There is always the risk that meditation programs in the classroom, while helpful in terms of getting the children to relax and quieten down, use elsewhere God language, as, for example, "Now imagine that God is looking over you lovingly. What do you want to say to God? Speak to God now in the silence." This traditional Christian language and imagery should be avoided in favor of mantras or phrases that affirm the presence of the Divine here and now.

Formal Prayer

Breaking life-long habits of praying to an elsewhere, listening God presents a significant challenge. As we seek to pray in new ways that reflect the "new story" about God and ourselves, we struggle for words and images. The following simple pattern may be helpful here:

1. Affirmation of the divine Presence,

2. Gratitude for how that Presence has been revealed to us,

3. Acknowledgement that everyone and everything is connected in this Presence.

4. Expression of the desires or hopes of the people praying,

5. Personal commitment to giving best-possible expression to this Presence.

These steps need not be present in every prayer, but can form the basis of a pattern that may be used with children and with people of all ages for many occasions, for example, prayer before a class, prayer before a meeting, prayer for parents, prayer for someone on their birthday, prayer before meals, prayer for peace in our world, prayer after sharing the daily news, prayer for the earth, prayer for people who are suffering, and so on.

This prayer format is faithful to the example of Jesus and the great Christian mystics in that it focuses strongly on remembrance, affirmation and commitment. Remembrance: tell the stories of God-with-us for they are the stories to sustain us. Affirmation: so central to Jesus' teaching about the "kingdom" of God in our midst. Commitment: we must *be* neighbor to one another, across all cultural and ethnic and religious boundaries. Commitment is *the* test of all prayer, for what use is whatever we do in "prayer" if we act unkindly or unjustly towards one another?

Some of the prayers that follow have a wish component. While "wish" may conjure up magic and the impossible and fairies or whatever, children can quickly learn that "wish" here has a definite meaning. Perhaps it could be linked with prayer and used as a specific term, as in "prayer wish". What is a "prayer wish"? It is an expression of our hopes and desires, voiced in the belief that everyone and everything is connected in the mystery we call God and that this Presence at work in our lives can do more than we ask or imagine. If we educate children in this conviction, it could then become a matter of course to ask, for example, what is our "prayer wish" for Maryanne or for the world or for someone who is sick? Initially, children might "wish" the totally unreal, but with some guidance they will learn that what we are looking for should be reasonable or hopeful.

The following prayers model the pattern described above. Using this prayer format may seem somewhat stilted at first but frequent practice will help words and phrases to flow more readily. The examples are not offered in the expectation that they will be used word for word. Rather they are offered as a model that may be helpful when leading children into formal prayer that does not address an elsewhere deity.

Ω: Prayer for someone who is sick.

Whether the prayer takes place in a classroom setting or at home, have all present hold hands. Begin by drawing attention to the holding of hands and the connectedness with one another.

Just as we hold hands and feel we are all connected with one another, we believe that everything is connected and held in existence by God.

God is everywhere, all through our universe, like a spirit breathing life and energy into everything.

We give thanks for all the ways we see the spirit and presence of God at work in our beautiful world and in our families and friends.

We pray for Maryanne.

May she draw strength and healing from God's presence with her and from our prayers and thoughts for her.

May she have peace in her heart and know she is greatly loved by us and her family and friends.

Let us now be quiet for a few moments and think of Maryanne.

Let us be aware that we are connected with Maryanne through God's presence.

What is your prayer wish for Maryanne?

(Some moments of silence)

We offer our prayers today believing that God's presence and power can do more than we can ever know.

Amen.

Ω: Prayer at the Beginning of the School Day

We give thanks for the Spirit of God present in our world and present here in each one of us.

We give thanks for the ways we see the Spirit of God present to us in people who love us and care for us.

We give thanks for the special abilities and talents each one of us has: they are gifts of God's Spirit with us.

May the Spirit of God be seen in all we do and say and learn today.

Amen.

Ω: A Birthday Blessing

Mary, we love all the ways we see the Spirit of God in you.

We see God's Spirit in the way you smile, your readiness to help, the way you play, the way you share.

You are a delight to us and you make God seem close to us because we see God's Spirit alive in you.

Today, on your birthday, we want you to know you are a treasure to us and we love you greatly because you are you, just the way you are.

Our birthday wish and blessing is:

Be happy, knowing you are greatly loved and knowing that God is always in your heart and in your life.

Amen.

Ω: Prayer for Peace

We believe that God's Spirit is in everyone.

We believe that God's Spirit is seen when people love and care and when they try to be neighbor to one another.

We believe that God's Spirit is blocked when people hurt one another and when they turn to violence and war.

We pray that people everywhere will listen to the presence of God's Spirit in them and that they will respect the presence of God's Spirit in other people.

We pray that war and violence and hatred will come to an end.

We commit ourselves to respecting God's presence in other people and to being peace-makers.

Amen.

Ω: Death of a School Friend

It is presumed that there has been time for conversation and sharing about the child's death before prayer begins. It could also be helpful for children to paint or draw or write as a means to express their feelings and ideas about death.

Everyone present hold hands.

Just as we hold hands and are all connected with one another, we believe that everything in our world and in our universe is connected through God's presence.

Even when people die, they are still connected with us and with God in ways we cannot see.

We do not believe that death is the end of Nathan.

We believe that Nathan lives on in God's Presence and that there is no pain and no suffering in that Presence, only a peace that is better than we can ever know.

We give thanks for Nathan's friendship with us.

We give thanks especially for the way he ...

(Give the child or children a chance to share.)

Many people are sad and feeling a great sense of loss because of Nathan's death.

Let us pray for them, since we believe we are connected with them, just as we are holding hands here with one another...

Let us pray quietly for Nathan's parents, his brothers, John and Paul, and for Stacey, his sister...

And now let us pray quietly for those of us who are most saddened by Nathan's death...

We offer these prayers believing that Nathan, his family and friends and all of us are somehow still together in God's presence.

May that presence of God help all of us to deal with Nathan's death.

Amen.

Ω: Prayer for the Earth

This prayer could follow class discussion on how we can care for the earth and the environment. Make a list of suggestions.

We believe God's Spirit has always been present on earth since its beginning.

We believe God's Spirit was present and active

in the first signs of life on land and in the sea,

and in the millions and millions of years during which plants and animals developed.

We believe that God's Spirit and the earth

brought human life into existence,

so we respect the earth and God's Spirit present here.

We pray that people everywhere will care for and look after our planet so that it will continue to be healthy and life-giving.

We will do all we can to help by ...

(Mention some of the suggestions listed.)

May earth be blessed by our actions.

Amen.

Prayers like these arise from the "new story" about our universe, about God presence throughout the universe and about Jesus revealing God's presence to us. This "new story" radically impinges on how we pray, how we worship and how we engage sacramental rituals. It leads us to question traditional approaches to prayer and theological thinking. Yet, if we face the challenges and persevere in our efforts to help children pray a "new story" we will bring them closer to the essence of Jesus' teaching and his hopes for humanity than many of us acquired in childhood. Most importantly, they will gain a sense of loving intimacy with the Divine Presence which will challenge them to be the best possible personal expressions of that Presence. If we adult educators work at it, think it through and use this "new story" wisely in educating the young, the future Church will have a wonderful message to offer the world – even if it has taken us 2000 years to reclaim what set Jesus' heart on fire.

Chapter Six

Feast Days: Celebrating
the Divine Presence

Christmas

Christmas should be the story of a Divine Presence that permeates the universe and came to human expression in Jesus. Look at any baby and consider that this baby is the product of atoms in transformation on this planet for four and a half billion years. Consider that this baby is stardust transformed beyond stardust, that this baby will give the universe itself a way to reflect and to love and to laugh. Consider that this baby has come to expression *in* and *through* the activity and presence we call God. Christmas, then, should not the story of an elsewhere God coming to expression in only one human being. The reality to which Christmas points is far more wonderful than that: all things and all people give expression to the mystery we call God.

The Christmas story is meant to mirror what Jesus' own preaching manifested: the Divine comes to expression in the most unlikely places. Jesus preached this Good News to the downtrodden, to the "sinners" and to anyone who thought that God could not be close to them. This story highlights a simple couple, a backward village, a repressed people and a "stable". The Divine is to be recognized in such places and in such people. This is the theme of the

Christmas story. It goes hand in hand with one of the great themes in the Old Testament: God delights to work with nothingness and through the weak. The stories of creation, Abraham and Sarah, Moses, the Covenant and the prophets (for example, the story of Gideon – the youngest in the lowest clan) all carry the theme of a God who chooses to work with the powerless rather than the high and the mighty. The New Testament carries the same theme when it tells the story of the elderly Zachary and his barren wife becoming the parents of John the Baptist and the story of a young "virgin" becoming the mother of Jesus.

Christmas should not be the story of a first time event, as if God, after a long absence, came to this planet in the form of Jesus. Our Christmas story must honor the reality of the Divine Presence all through the four and a half billion years of earth's history. It must honor and appreciate and give credence to the development of the human species and all other life forms *in* God *always here.*

The heart of prayer leading to Christmas should be gratitude for this particular baby who has shown people how close God is to all of us. People did not realize God was with them in their everyday lives and in their caring. They thought they were not holy or religious enough for that. Jesus wanted to change that thinking and to show that God is very close to all of us.

This is what we give thanks for at Christmas – the birth, the life and the preaching of Jesus who wants us to see that the Divine is in all of us. It is also why we sing carols and rejoice and call Jesus Savior – because he has set us free from fear of God and ideas that God is far away.

The Divine comes to unique expression in each and every person. No two people are identical in the way they give expression to God's presence in their lives. We can appreciate this in the ways people are gifted with their own particular talents and abilities. The topic of gifts is never far from children's minds at this time of the year. We could encourage them to talk about gifts they have received for birthdays or Christmas in the past, which ones they most appreciated, what they are looking forward to receiving next Christmas.

We could then discuss with them another kind of gift – as in personal gifts. What does it mean to say that someone is a "gifted" person? The discussion will cover abilities, talents, skills, qualities and aptitudes. Children could name the gifts of some people well-known in entertainment or sport or medicine or other fields of human endeavor.

What are the gifts obvious in students in this class?

In your best friends?

In your family members?

Where do these gifts come from?

They come from the Divine Presence in our lives. We all have our own particular gifts.

Let us then make this a theme of our Christmas story and reflection: giving thanks for the Divine Presence that permeates everyone and everything.

Encourage children to make their own Christmas cards for friends and family – and teacher. (Perhaps the teacher could make a card for each student as well.) Invite them to use the following example for writing a message inside the card:

Mary, I see the Divine expressed in you when you share, when you smile and when you invite other children into our games.

This exercise is a practical way of implementing Jesus' concern that people name the connection between their good deeds ("living in love") and God's presence with them ("living in God" and "God living in them"). The failure to constantly name and articulate that connection has been one of the greatest mistakes of the Christian religion. Christmas invites us to see the Divine Presence in the "stables", the ordinariness, of our own lives.

Advent

We have centuries of liturgical prayers highlighting "Come!" such as "Come Emmanuel, Come to us." Advent is usually seen as a preparation for Jesus' coming. A drawback with this focus in Advent is that it requires intellectual gymnastics: to pray as if Jesus has not yet come into the world or into our minds and hearts. It would be easier and better to focus on affirmation of the Divine Presence with us and gratitude for Jesus as revealer of that Presence.

Ω: Advent prayer

We give thanks that God is everywhere and in all people.

We give thanks for Jesus who showed us that God is with us in all we do.

We believe that God is with us in our giftedness and in the giftedness of our friends and families.

We will respect our differences as Jesus would want us to.

We want Christmas to be a happy time for everyone because it is a special time for loving and giving and we know our loving and giving express God's presence with us.

(Pause and invite children to name people they want to remember and pray for.)

We celebrate the birth of Jesus with joy because he showed us how close God is to us.

We pray that people everywhere will recognize God's closeness to them and will allow God's presence to be seen in the way they celebrate Christmas with one another.

Amen.

Holy Thursday

Traditional Christian teaching would have us believe that on the night before he died Jesus ordained his apostles priests and instituted the Eucharist as we know it today. This is what many of us were taught at an early age and grew into adulthood believing without question. The majority of adult Catholics still would not question it.

As educators of young children about the "last supper" of Jesus, our task is twofold. First, to be clear in our own minds what the significance of this meal is after we free it from the layers of later theological interpretation. Second, to be clear what we want to teach children about it.

When we get below the layers of theological interpretation about this meal we are confronted with the reality that Jesus was a Jew who never renounced his religion. We need to be very clear about this. The earliest Christians were Jews who went "as a body to the temple every day". (Acts 3:46) Paul, Peter, James, John and the other apostles along with Mary, the mother of Jesus, never renounced their Judaism. The break of the Christian "religion" from Judaism took place more than thirty years after Jesus died. This historical fact was generally ignored in what most of us learned as young children. We were taught that Jesus wanted to start a new religion before he died and did so at the last supper when he ordained his apostles. This is not the case. Jesus never "ordained" anyone. He did not begin a new religion separate from Judaism.

The heart of the meal Jesus had with his friends the night before he died, if it was a Passover meal, was "Remember, remember, remember!" Remember the times of slavery and hardship. Remember how God set us free. Remember how God sustained and fed us in the desert. Remember that God is always with us.

In this context, Jesus asked his Jewish friends to remember him in a special way whenever they gathered in the future – as Jews naturally – to share this meal. Jesus was asking his followers to put him in this story of God at work with the Jewish people. He wanted them to remember him as someone who gave his all (bread broken and shared) for a covenant of love rather than law. He wanted them to commit themselves to living and loving as he had. He wanted them to ritualize this commitment, to give their "Yes" in the act of eating and drinking.

While it is true that young children can have difficulty with symbolic language, it is worthwhile to discuss symbols and gestures and rituals with which they are familiar. For example, why do married people wear weddings rings? Why do people shake hands? Does the school or a club to which they belong or which they support have a special symbol? What does a flag symbolize? Symbols are important because they have special meaning for people within a group. They are a way of keeping deeply respected, important truths before our eyes. They help bind a group together. They carry meaning and value for people. They are useful because they become familiar to and are easily recognized by members of a group. With this discussion as background, share with children why the Jewish people considered the Passover Meal to be so important. The food and drink at the meal were intrinsically linked with remembering: bitter herbs – the tough times; bread – sustenance from God on the journey, wine – a covenant sealed with the sprinkling of blood; eating – "com-union", the way everyone present gave their assent to what was asked.

A crucial question for Jesus at this moment of his life was: What am I ready to die for? As educators we should articulate for ourselves how we imagine Jesus would respond to that question. For example, do we imagine him thinking he was ready to die in order to open the gates of heaven because an elsewhere God had denied access to the Divine presence? Did he think he was dying for "the sins of the world" and that his death would restore friendship between the human species and God? Or did this Jewish man not think in these terms and concepts at all? Could it be that he was ready to die for what he believed and taught: that God's presence is accessible to everyone in their everyday living and loving?

What, then, will we focus on when we talk with children about Holy Thursday?

When we link the events of this night to Jesus' preaching, rather than to a later theological construct, Jesus' actions fall into place. He knew he would soon be arrested and that he was very likely going to die. He wanted his disciples to follow in his footsteps and keep his dream alive. They were to do this by keeping alive his freeing, insightful Good News about God's presence with people and by being of service to people. Jesus realized that if his apostles became rulers over people they would forget the heart of his message. That is why he washed their feet.

How do we be of service to one another in the way Jesus wanted? How does Mom do it for the family? How does Dad do it? Our brothers, sisters, teachers, friends? Politicians? Other people in society? How can we do it for one another? In these ways we can be "the body of Christ" for one another. That is where the emphasis should be –

not on Jesus *in* the bread and how that can happen and who has special power to make it happen.

With children, we should avoid as much as possible theological issues such as how does Jesus get into the bread or how the bread becomes his "body" – even if the Religious Education curriculum focuses on these issues. These were not issues at the Last Supper. In the later section on Eucharist emphasis will be placed more on what we are ritualizing about our readiness to say "Yes" (Amen) to Jesus rather than on the bread and how it is "transformed" into the "body" of Jesus.

Ω: Holy Thursday Prayer

We give thanks for the Jewish people and the way they constantly remembered God.

We give thanks for Jesus and his preaching that God is with us in our loving.

We give thanks that he was ready to die for what he believed.

We want to say "Yes" to his invitation to keep his dream for our world alive.

We give thanks that the Spirit of God that moved in Jesus' life is with us as we try to keep his dream alive.

May we show the presence of God's Spirit in us in all we do and say.

Amen.

Good Friday

Good Friday in a "new story" about our universe should be freed from belief that an external God wanted a price to be paid in order for humanity to regain access to his presence. Such an idea belongs within a theological construct that views God as a deity who required compensation for having being wronged. It does not fit either with Jesus' preaching about God nor with a contemporary understanding of God as a universal Presence.

Jesus preached that the Divine is to be found everywhere, in the poor and the lowly, the sick and the despised, in ordinary people struggling to make ends meet, in people who thought the Divine could not be anywhere near them and in everyone who acts lovingly.

Good Friday is the story of this Jewish man who was ready to die for what he believed. It is a story of faith in the face of apparent hopelessness. It is the story of a man who stood by his convictions despite the consequences.

Some people will object that we are reducing Jesus' death to the realm of the merely human. They fear we are taking away any sense of his divinity.

The objection stems from centuries of attributing a special kind of divinity to Jesus because he died for our sins and won back friendship with God. That theological thinking required Jesus to be identified with God in a way the rest of us are not. However, if we were never cut off from God in the first place, if it was ignorance of God's presence with us that Jesus helped us overcome, not actual separation from God (since that is an impossibility!), then Jesus rightly belongs with all of humanity in being permeated with God's presence. It is precisely his attentiveness to the Divine Presence in himself that alerted him to the same Divine Presence in all people and motivated him to preach that Good News.

In the way Jesus died for what he believed we see the nobility of the human spirit. When we see expressions of human nobility and love, we Christians, inspired by Jesus' teaching and example, identify the human spirit with the "spirit" of God at work. We have seen this human/divine spirit in our friends and relations as they too have faced adversity and death. It is our task to recognize and name the connection – human spirit: spirit of God. We need to nurture this awareness rather than be caught into a theological mind-set that insists on telling us that only Jesus is *really* divine.

When talking to children about Good Friday we should draw attention to what Jesus believed in spite of suffering and a cruel death. What must it have been like for Jesus to be falsely accused and have to stand up for what he believed?

Ask children if they have ever been accused of doing something they never did. Explore with them how hard it is sometimes to do what is right when other people want you to go against your belief.

In the lead-up to Holy Week, explore with children stories about men and women prepared to suffer for their beliefs or for what is right. Focus on who benefited and how people were helped or encouraged by their example. Affirm the Divine Presence at work in these people.

Ask children to name other people they know who give wonderful, insightful, courageous expression to this presence.

Good Friday is also a special occasion for remembering people close to us who have died in the past year. Encourage children to speak about people they know who have died, their good qualities and how they helped people. Focus on how their goodness lives on in our memories of them and inspires us to do good.

With regard to the physical aspects of Jesus' death, yes, tell the story of the crown of thorns, Jesus being whipped and made fun of, carrying his cross and dying in pain. However, be sure, very sure, not to give the impression that Jesus' suffering was a price he had to pay for our sins. What we want to draw from reflection on Jesus' suffering and death is what he would want us to believe about life, love and God and the way we relate with one another. What would he say to us? What would he say to people who are themselves suffering?

The ritual of kissing the cross is a focal gesture in traditional Good Friday liturgy. Many people will kiss the cross in thanksgiving for Jesus dying for their sins and winning access to heaven. If children are to participate in this ritual, encourage them to focus on the gesture as their way of saying "Yes" to Jesus' invitation to share his faith and to keep his dream alive by doing good or as a gesture of thanks to Jesus for showing us how close God is to each of us.

Ω: Good Friday Prayer

We give thanks for the life of Jesus

and for all he taught about God being with us

when we care for and love one another.

We give thanks for his courage –

he never gave up believing what he taught,

even when people were cruel to him.

We pray that we and all people

will hear the message of Jesus

and live in such a way

that what Jesus did not see in his lifetime

might be seen in our lifetime –

people trusting the power of love and generosity

more than the power of greed and selfishness.

Like Jesus, we want to be strong in standing up for what we believe to be true and good.

Today, as we remember Jesus suffering,

we also remember people in our world

who are sad or lonely or suffering

or who feel that God is not close to them.

We give thanks for our friends and relatives who have died.

They have helped us by the way they loved and cared for people.

They showed the presence of God in their actions.

May their goodness live on in our lives in the way we care for one another.

We pray especially for ...

(Ask children to name people or groups)

We pray that all people might know that God is close to them. Amen.

Easter and Ascension

Easter deals with the *mystery* of death and the good news that death is not the end of us. We have no images that can even remotely deal with the question of what lies beyond death for us. It is well that we keep this in mind, otherwise we make the mistake of literalizing images that belong to ancient notions of the cosmos and of a journey to a deity who lives in the heavens. Most of Christian liturgy, ritual and prayers dealing with death are shaped in this outmoded cosmological and religious worldview. We continue to literalize Gospel stories of Jesus "rising" and "ascending into heaven" as if he went up to that somewhere else place where God really dwells. The Creed and Catechism and Christian preaching invoke the same images and language. It is not surprising, therefore, that Christians generally have not stopped to question what traditional Christian teaching has led them to believe and imagine about death being a journey to where God is.

God is not somewhere else. Let us be clear about this and bring our clarity to the task of reflecting on these feast days. We are not celebrating or understanding the "resurrection" of Jesus in the same worldview as the Scripture writers understood it and wrote about it. We are not imagining it the way Christian tradition has imagined and interpreted it. Those influences locked Christians into thinking and imagining that Easter is primarily about God raising Jesus, taking him to heaven, granting him the fullness of God's Spirit, releasing the Spirit on the followers of Jesus, and granting humanity access to God because of Jesus' fidelity to whatever God asked of him.

This traditional Christian thinking is grounded in concepts of an elsewhere God denying access to himself as if everyone who lived before Jesus died into a state of separation from God. That thinking is a denial of Jesus' own teaching concerning the intimate link between living in love and living in God. If living in love is intrinsically connected with living in God then everyone who lived before Jesus lived and died *in* God.

Children will inevitably be subjected to the language and imagery of disconnectedness from God and of Jesus as the unique person who won back connectedness for us – just as we were throughout our lives. It will often be taught and preached as reality. Educators immersed in a new story about God and the universe will want to counterbalance traditional Christian thinking about:

- A God who denied access to himself because of a human being's sin.

- Heaven as an elsewhere place

- Jesus gained access to that place by his obedience – or by his dying on a cross for our sins.

- An elsewhere God "raising" Jesus and taking him "up" into heaven.

- Easter as a grand, first time event celebrating human access to God after death – only through Jesus' death.

- Judgment by God as to who "enters heaven" or not.

- Entrance into this place through membership of a particular religion.

The counterbalance educators seek will be achieved by emphasizing the following:

- The universality of the Divine Presence, a presence permeating all that is.

- Jesus as revealer of that presence in all people, not someone who gains unique access to God or the one who restores friendship with God.

- Death as a transformation of the way we exist *in* God rather than a journey to an elsewhere deity who will make a solemn judgment about whether we will enter his presence or not.

- Mystery. We have no images of what happens after death, but we believe that death is not the end of us.

- We are not to fear death.

- Jesus' preaching about death that we can draw from: the parables of the Prodigal Son and the vineyard workers who worked the shortest hours. Death will be *like* embracing the most loving, gracious, forgiving, extraordinarily generous person imaginable.

- Everyone who has ever lived on this planet has lived – and died – *in* God.

- The interconnectedness of all things does not cease when anyone or anything dies.

Images of Winter and Spring may be used to help children develop a wholesome attitude to death and whatever is beyond. In Winter, so much around us seems to die, then in Spring it all bursts into new life. Death is like that. Yes, we will die, and this human way of existing will come to an end, but we believe there is a new life beyond what we can experience now. It is just as mysterious as contemplating what seems to be a lifeless tree in the middle of Winter and then seeing it bud and blossom in Spring.

At Easter, reflection on the wonder of the seasonal changes and how they manifest the cycle of birth, life, death, and new life can lead can lead to an appreciation of our own transformation and rebirth *in* God.

Easter is an opportunity to widen our story about God's wonderful, mysterious presence on this planet, in all living things, in us, and throughout the universe. This is a far better story than a story that fixates on God's presence in heaven and how access is gained to that presence only through Jesus. And there is little doubt about which story Jesus himself would tell!

When we use the Gospel stories about Jesus appearing to people after he died, we should point out that these stories were a way of saying that even though Jesus had died, people believed he was still with them in some way. Not only was he still with them, he was also with God in a new way. This is how it will be for all of us. As educators we need to be mindful that these Gospel stories are myth. They are not meant to be interpreted literally. Myth deals with mystery and meaning beyond what our words and images can apprehend or convey. The greatest mystery we face in life is death – and what lies beyond. These post-Easter stories point to an insight and belief that are good news: death is not the end; in death we are transformed into a new way of living on *in* God.

The story of the Ascension should be told with the explanation that at the time of Jesus people believed that God lived above the earth. When they wanted to convey that Jesus was with God, they expressed their belief through the story of an "ascension" that entailed Jesus going up from the earth. The story was their way of dealing with the mystery of death: no one knows what actually happens when we die. When we hear this story today we should hear what the story is trying to tell us, that Jesus died into God's presence and lives on in a new way. The ascension should not be understood as an actual physical event. It is powerful myth dealing with a mystery beyond our comprehension. That is why we keep telling this story. If we literalize it, we destroy its power to communicate hope and meaning in the face of mystery; we simply make it unbelievable.

Ω: Easter Prayer

We give thanks for the wonderful world in which we live.

We give thanks that we are united with everything and everyone in God.

We give thanks that God's presence can be seen in the beauty of nature

and in the changing of the seasons.

We give thanks for Fall when ... (ask children to finish the sentence)

We give thanks for Winter when ...

We give thanks for Spring when ...

We give thanks for Summer when ...

We give thanks for Jesus who ...

We give thanks at Easter because ...

Most of all we rejoice and give thanks

that the same Spirit of Life

that moved in Jesus

moves in all of us.

We want that Spirit to live and love in us

as generously as it lived and loved in Jesus.

We pray that all Jesus dreamed for our world

may come true.

Amen.

Pentecost

Pentecost in traditional Christian theology is the story of God sending the Holy Spirit, the Spirit of God, upon the followers of Jesus as a consequence of Jesus' death, resurrection and ascension into heaven. It is the story of renewed contact and friendship with God through belief in Jesus as "savior" of the world. It is also the story of the birth of the Church and of the Church as the bearer of God's Spirit to the world.

The "new story" about God and our universe necessitates radical rethinking of this traditional Christian theological construct because it is cemented in ideas of separation from an elsewhere God and how access to that elsewhere God is won.

Our understanding of the universe and our respect for the universality of God's presence demand we take seriously that the Spirit of God, however we wish to conceive it, has always been present and active throughout the universe and on this planet. To imagine that the Spirit stayed, as it were, in heaven until Jesus died and was "taken up" into heaven is nonsensical today.

Children will read or be taught about the Neanderthals and the earliest Homo Sapiens. Was the Spirit of God present and active in these people? Yes, the Spirit was there, working in and through what it had to work with. Was the Spirit active and present in the development of language, the use of tools, art, and culture? Was the Spirit of God present and active in the human species when people first tried to give meaning to life and wondered where life came from, why things happened the way they did and what happens in death?

Was that Spirit present and active in the Australian aboriginal people 40,000 years ago in their exploration and settlement in a vast continent? Was it present and active in the First Nation people of Canada and other North American native people, working in and through their questions and their understanding of the cosmos and the world around them? Was it present and active in the people of China, India, South America, Asia, Africa, Europe and all around the world in the centuries before Jesus lived?

Was that Spirit present and active in the great religious leaders and thinkers who emerged well before Jesus such as Buddha, Confucius, Zoroaster, Plato, Socrates, and Aristotle?

Was the Divine Spirit present and active in Hosea, Jeremiah, Isaiah, Naomi, Ruth? Was not this same Spirit present and active in the Greeks, the Babylonians and the Romans, working through the limitations of their religious worldviews and understanding of the cosmos?

It is remarkable that on the one hand it seems so obvious to say "Yes" to all these questions, yet on the other, the link is so seldom made in religious educational processes. The reason for this failure doubtless has its roots in Christianity's traditional theology of "revelation" which emphasizes an elsewhere God intervening and communicating only through a chosen group. This theology benefits members of the chosen group but is a grave disservice to belief in God's constant, universal presence. What we inherited from this theology was the idea that "revelation" came from heaven "down" to us. This is still the only acceptable understanding of revelation for most branches of the Christian religion, especially in conservative circles and is evident in Vatican documents. This theological attitude closes minds to the obvious: that the Spirit of God has always been present in the slow development of the human species and that revelation is not a "heaven - down" phenomenon, but a "ground - up" one. In other words, our understanding of God, the Divine Presence, comes from the Divine Presence working within and among us rather than being the product of an elsewhere deity revealing "Himself" to a chosen group at a particular point in time.

Children should be introduced to the belief that the Divine Spirit works in and through the mentality, giftedness, and worldview of people at their time in history – in their stories, customs and religious laws.

With such grounding, children can be led to an appreciation of Bible stories about creation or why people speak different languages without literalizing those stories the way biblical fundamentalism insists they be understood.

Encourage children to collect, read and share stories of indigenous people around the world. Focus on stories connecting the land with the "Spirit of Life" or the "Great Spirit" or whatever term used to refer to a sacred, divine presence at work on earth. Isn't this the Spirit of God working in and through the people of the time? Encourage children to discover what is common to all people in how their stories encourage people to treat one another and to interact with the earth.

The next step is to bring these considerations to Jesus, his ministry and to our understanding of Pentecost.

Was the Spirit in all the people who gathered to hear Jesus? Yes, but that Spirit was limited by their ability to understand or appreciate what they were hearing. All their lives they had been led to think differently from what Jesus was teaching.

It was not any absence of God's Spirit that Jesus thought he was addressing; it was peoples' ignorance and blindness to the Divine Presence in the here and now. The Spirit was there all the while in peoples' lives but they did not recognize it. So Jesus taught people to open their eyes and minds to see their living and loving in a whole new light: *when you love, when you care, when you forgive, when you visit, when you clothe ... in all these everyday actions of yours, God is present and you are making the "reign" of God visible in the world.* The sacred was intimately present with them in their everyday activity but they could not "see" it or appreciate it because they had never been led to see the connection. We need to keep this teaching method of Jesus alive not only with regard to our own everyday activities, but also with regard to the children whose faith we aim to nurture.

Was the Spirit of God in people who opposed Jesus? Yes. This is an important issue to explore. Some people who opposed Jesus acted according to what they honestly believed to be right. The Spirit was present and active in them, working in and through their personalities and beliefs – just as it does with us today. Some people doubtlessly opposed Jesus for selfish reasons or through fear. The Spirit was also present in them but not able to be given worthwhile human expression because of the selfishness or fear.

After his death, people reflected on Jesus and came to see him as someone who allowed the Spirit of God to be expressed fully in human form. Awareness dawned on them: *Ah, we have seen more than just the human here. This man has shown us in his total dedication to love how God's Spirit and presence can be given expression in human form.* Then came the powerful, wonderful realization. *Ah, Jesus kept telling us that when we love, when we care and when we are generous, we too are connected with God; we live in God and God lives in us. And this is true for all people – of whatever religion, race or creed! This is the good news that unites all men and women! We do not have to be fearful of God or worry about who has access to God or who can bring us close to God – God is intimately close to all men and women when they live good and decent lives. Ah, now we see! We are temples of God's Spirit! We are* all *sacred! We earthen vessels hold a treasure! What good news for everyone! Let us now live this way!*

This was Jesus' vision, what he hoped people would realize.

The Pentecost question for children and for all of us to consider is: what difference would it make if everyone believed they and everyone else are sacred; that all people share in God's Spirit?

We can bring Jesus' method of instruction – linking everyday activity with the Divine Presence – to help children pray what Pentecost is meant to celebrate: that the Spirit of God is always active in our world and in our lives. We can do this at home or with students in a classroom. At home, ask children in a night prayer session where they have experienced goodness, love, kindness and sharing during the day. Lead the children into prayer by linking these experiences with the activity of the Spirit of God in their lives. Or, if the children are older, be more direct by asking them, *"Where and in whom did you see the Spirit of God present and active today?"* They may need some prompting, but if we are sure in our own minds that the Spirit of God is manifested in beauty, goodness, truth, care and generosity, we will readily help children to see the connection.

In a classroom setting, a litany form of prayer may be used to reinforce understanding and awareness that God's Spirit is always and universally present. Ask the children to reflect on the universe and its formation and/ or the wonders of this planet and/or the development of human life and/or what they have experienced in the past week and/or life at home ... the variations are endless! Ask each child to have one item in mind that highlights the presence of the Spirit of God.

In the prayer time the students all say together:

Ω: Pentecost Prayer

We see the Spirit of God present and active...

(Students in turn finish with statements they have prepared, such as:)

... in the billions and billions of years it took the galaxies to form.

... in the beauty of nature.

... in my parents' generosity and care for me.

... in my friend's courage.

... in the stranger who helped my Dad.

Chapter Seven

The Sacraments: Ritualizing the Divine Presence

Older generations of Catholics are accustomed to thinking of sacraments as rituals that either bring God's presence or grant access to God. The sacrament of priesthood plays a major role since it alone grants the power to specially trained men to operate the sacramental system.

Jesus, however, would find our sacramental system very strange and quite contrary to his basic teaching about discovering the presence of God in our everyday activities.

It is too easy for us – and too convenient for institutional Church leadership – to forget or overlook Jesus' approach to his own religious system. He was so radical that he became a threat to the system. Why? Because he insisted that people could discover and celebrate the sacred in their everyday living and loving instead of being dependent on a priestly caste to access the sacred. Such preaching – and we know it is what Jesus stood for – was and still remains a threat to a priestly or institutional leadership system that claims authority and power over access to the sacred. It is subversive of established religious order, authority and power because it gives power and authority and dignity to everyone. Jesus made it clear that this was something to rejoice over, like someone finding a treasure

(Mt 13:44). This was the "good news" he wanted people to believe.

Jesus would undoubtedly be puzzled that a religion bearing his name would encase itself in a sacramental system that makes people dependent on middle management to access the sacred. He would surely be disturbed by the way the Catholic Church for the past thousand years has insisted that only Baptism grants access to "God's life and grace", that only Confirmation brings "the gifts of the Spirit", that only through the sacrament of Reconciliation can we have assurance of God's forgiveness, that only the "sacrament of matrimony" opens a couple to God's presence in their marriage, and that the sacraments of Priesthood and Eucharist are so fixated on powers to "bring" God's Presence to people.

Jesus would surely want to point out that his preaching gives no support to such thinking.

Jesus appreciated the value of ritual and sacrament since he obviously participated in the Jewish liturgical rituals such as the Passover and going to the Temple. However, he would remind us that the Passover meal, on which we model our Eucharistic celebrations, focused on God's presence and activity in the past and God's presence and activity in the here and now. It was not concerned with who had special powers to bring God's Presence to the gathering.

We can imagine that Jesus would invite us to look again at our sacraments and to consider them in the light of his insistence that the sacred is here with us rather than an entity to be brought from elsewhere through the use of prayer and ritual.

To accept such an invitation from Jesus is a daunting task, very similar to the one Jesus faced in his public ministry. We are likely to face the same sort of religious opposition he faced because the stakes are high. Yet it must be done if we are to nurture children into a religious lifestyle that is modeled on the teaching of Jesus rather than on an ecclesial system intent on preserving its power and its authority over people.

When introducing children to the Church's key sacraments, it is important, then, that our starting point and primary focus throughout should be the teaching of Jesus about the presence of God with us and how we might ritualize, celebrate and say "yes" to this Presence in our lives. In doing so, it is inevitable that we notice, perhaps surprisingly, that this is not the approach taken in most Roman Catholic educational materials on the sacraments.

It is also important to keep in mind that sacraments were initially adult realities. Baptism and Eucharist, the two key sacraments for most Christians, were originally grounded on adult commitment to following Jesus and his teaching. The focus and practice of Baptism changed dramatically 1500 years ago when St Augustine's teaching on original sin shifted attention to the baptism of babies. The primary concern of baptismal practice then became the removal of the "stain" of original sin and ensuring a place in heaven if the child were to die. Infant baptism was not, and could not be, concerned with personal choice and commitment. The focus on the sacrament concentrated on what it "did", what its "effects" were, and who could make the sacrament "work".

A similar shift occurred with Eucharistic thought and practice. Early in the twentieth century Pius X enabled children to receive Communion more readily and frequently. However, while this change was greatly appreciated throughout the Church, it further embedded in popular Catholic thought the medieval idea that the sacrament is primarily about "reception" rather than personal commitment to *"be"* the "Body of Christ". The focus has been, and still is, on a "real" presence, how the sacrament works and who has the power to make it work.

Our thinking and teaching about the sacraments will be enriched if we keep two factors in mind. First, the sacraments should be seen as actions, symbols and words that ritualize our belief in God-with-us and challenge us to give witness to that Presence in the way we live. They are not rituals accessing God's Presence, even though many Catholics have been led to believe that is their purpose. Sacraments must be viewed in the understanding that God's presence permeates all that is, rather than in the dualistic worldview of traditional Catholic thought that separates heaven and earth. Second, while we may be very familiar with what is considered to be the "tradition" for understanding and participating in the sacraments (as if this is the only way they have always been understood), there are other traditions in early Church history. For example,

- Individual "confession" with absolution by a priest did not exist in the Church for 600 years and was banned by the Church when it first appeared. The early tradition of the Church emphasized the community's role in forgiving or not forgiving public sinners. The permission of the community for the sinner to return to the Eucharist was the most essential part of the reconciling process.

- Baptism ritualized adult personal commitment centuries before concern about original sin changed it predominantly to a ritual to ensure that infants who died would get to heaven.

- Early Eucharistic thinking and practice, while venerating the consecrated bread, gave as much if not more emphasis to the people being "the Body of Christ". The people's "Amen" response at communion was their acknowledgement of who they were.

- In the early Church priesthood was not so much concerned with liturgy and celibacy and special powers, but more with community leadership. It was unthinkable to have a community leader and Eucharistic presider who did not emerge from the community itself.

- Confirmation was not a separate sacrament for the first four hundred years. It was a part of the baptismal ceremony.

The treatment of Baptism, Confirmation, Reconciliation and Eucharist in the following pages will explore some of these earlier beliefs and practices that have been overshadowed and will incorporate them into a contemporary understanding of these sacraments. Only the four sacraments closest to children's experience will be examined.

Baptism

What might a baptismal ceremony look like if it avoided the dualism and the Fall/Redemption language of traditional Christian services?

For a start, it would avoid any reference to the ritual bringing "new life" or "taking away sin" or making the baptized "a child of God".

It would avoid prayers addressed to an elsewhere God.

It would affirm universal connectedness with the Mystery we call "God".

It would affirm the sacredness of human love.

It would mirror Jesus' words and actions by urging parents and family to recognize their intimate connectedness with God in and through their love.

When talking to children about baptism the focus should be on rejoicing in God's presence in this infant. This is not a ritual that brings God's presence. Every baby is born within God's presence. The words and actions are designed to express belief in that presence, not to bring it. The concern of the participants in the ritual – parents, sponsors, family and friends – should be on how that divine presence will be recognized and nurtured in the life of the child.

Both instruction about and the actual ritual of baptism should incorporate the contemporary story about our universe and the wonder of new life on this planet. We need this story to counterbalance the traditional baptismal story about a fall from God's grace. The "new story" tells of atoms manufactured in an exploding star four and a half billion years ago that now have taken shape in this new life. It tells of the wonder and the incomprehensibility of a Divine Presence at work in the vastness of our universe, a Presence that holds and sustains everything in existence and now comes to visible expression in this child. It declares the good news that we are a conscious life-form that gives "God" a way of coming to expression. It expresses the Wow! of human life. It gives a solid and worthwhile grounding in a spirituality that will resonate easily with the teaching of Jesus about God-with-us in all we do. It has the capacity to heal the harm done by a long tradition that insisted babies are born alienated from God, "poor, banished children of Eve."

The story will also challenge the hearers to be aware that they have the responsibility of being the presence of that same God for this child, as parent, as sponsor, as brother or sister or cousin or aunt, uncle or family friend.

Adults preparing for a family baptism ceremony can incorporate ways for children to be involved in the ceremony.

Children, especially brothers and sisters and cousins of the child being baptized should be encouraged to compose a prayer for the Prayers of the Faithful. Such prayers should avoid the "Dear God, please ..." pattern. Instead they should express something of the child's wish for the baby, for example, "We pray that Michele Jane will always have good health and know she is greatly loved." The point of the prayers is to express our desires and hopes, not to ask an elsewhere God to "grant" or "do" something.

Alternatively, older children could be asked to compose prayers they would like to read at the baptismal ceremony, prayers that link belief about God's presence with what they would wish for the child. Prayers of belief could use a statement-response format such as the following example:

Ω: Prayers of Belief

We believe that every child born into this world is a child of God.

We want to baptise Michele Jane in this belief.

We believe that God's presence and activity are shown in the love Michele Jane's parents and family have for her.

We want to baptise Michele Jane in this belief.

We believe that the life and teaching of Jesus set us free from fear of God.

We want to baptise Michele Jane in this belief.

We believe that when we love one another, God is close to us.

We want to baptise Michele Jane in this belief.

Such prayers can readily be added to the prayers that adults might shape at a baptismal ceremony, for example,

We believe that the Church exists to affirm God's loving presence with us and to challenge us to give witness to this presence in our love for one another.

We want to baptise Michele Jane in this belief.

Early in the ceremony children could be invited to come forward to touch or bless the baby in the belief that their touch and presence are ways God has of touching and being present to the baby.

The traditional elements of the baptismal ritual – the pouring of the water, the anointing, the baptismal candle and the white garment – will still be used, but in ways that express the "new story" understanding of God and our connectedness with God. All aspects of the ceremony should be consistent with and expressive of belief that God's presence with the baby is not dependent either on the ceremony itself or the words and actions used in the ceremony. For example, the words at the pouring of water should be an affirmation of the Divine Presence rather than a formula that people believe brings God's Presence.

Ω: Prayer at the pouring of water

Michele Jane, you are an earthen vessel holding a treasure.

You give God a way of coming to expression.

You live in God and God lives in you.

We baptise you into this faith

[pour water]

- *in the name of a God who is Source of all*
- *in the name of a God revealed in our own humanity*
- *in the name of a God of Life and Love*

If the presiding priest is unwilling to accommodate such changes, then parents and sponsors could seek to incorporate the above words and ritual into the ceremony following the priest's usage of the Church's official and "valid" baptismal formula.

When children – and parents, sponsors and grandparents – appreciate both the Divine Presence within the child being baptised and his or her connection with billions of years of the universe's development, then the traditional ritual elements of anointing, being clothed in a white garment and receiving a lighted candle take on added significance.

Why is the baby anointed? Oil has long been used throughout human history to signify the presence of the sacred. It would be appropriate if the prayer used at the anointing of the baby focused on this. The presider could pray, for example,

Ω: Prayer at the Anointing with Oil

Michele Jane, you were conceived in love and welcomed to life with love.

We anoint you with this oil in recognition that human love is sacred, that you are sacred.

May the presence of the Spirit of Love in you be nurtured and constantly affirmed by your family, by your friends and by the Church community.

Amen.

The gesture of presenting the baby with a white garment or a stole can also be linked prayerfully to the Divine

Presence. The godparents (and the grandparents also) could pray, for example,

Ω: Prayer at Presentation of White Garment

Michele Jane, we present you with this garment.

May it be a reminder throughout life that you carry in the depths of your being, in your loving and in all that makes you who you are, the Spirit of Life and Love itself.

Amen.

A baptismal candle is lit from the Easter candle and presented to the baby. The sponsors could do this and pray, for example:

Ω: Prayer when Baptismal Candle is Presented

Michele Jane, may this candle remind you of Jesus who opened peoples' minds and hearts to see the "light" of God's presence within them.

May his teaching and example enlighten you to walk humbly and confidently with your God throughout life and may it challenge you to allow the light of God's presence to shine in you.

Amen.

Ω: Blessing Prayers

The baptismal ceremony concludes with the presider

blessing the parents, then all present.

For the parents:

We rejoice, Mary and John, in seeing the Spirit of God, the Spirit of Love and Life, in your love for each other, your love for your family and your love for your friends.

We gladly join with you today in giving thanks for the wonderful gift of your shared love, Michele Jane, whom we have just baptized.

I bless you in the name of your friends and in the name of the Church community + and I pray with your family and friends that you will continue to be richly blessed in the fruits of love, knowing that the Source of all Love lives in you.

Amen.

For those present:

We are blessed in being here today.

We are blessed in knowing Mary and John.

And what a blessing it is to see this beautiful baby, Michele Jane.

A ceremony like this today touches us with the wonder and the joy of the Spirit of God, the Spirit of Life present and active in our living and loving.

Let us carry this blessing + in our hearts and minds and be thankful for life and love and family and friends.

Amen.

Confirmation

Confirmation as a separate sacrament is an historical accident. The gesture of "confirming" was originally part of the baptismal ceremony which was always celebrated by a bishop. It became separated in the fifth century as a result of Augustine's teaching on original sin. Jesus would surely have been greatly surprised at the idea that babies are born into a state of separation from God, but Augustine's theology of original sin locked this idea into Christian thought and practice. The high infant mortality rate at the time drove an urgent need to baptize babies before they died. This led to bishops delegating the act of baptizing to priests while retaining their role of "confirming" the sacrament. Because it took bishops months and sometimes years to visit each town and village, this resulted in "Confirmation" eventually becoming a separate sacrament.

Centuries later, the sacramental theology of the Middle Ages began to focus on the sacrament with questions such as, "How does this sacrament work?", "Who has the power to perform it?" and "What does this sacrament do or bring?" In our Catholic education we learned that only Bishops could perform the sacrament of Confirmation, that it made us "soldiers of Christ" and brought us the seven gifts of the Holy Spirit. Supposedly, even before we reached our teens, we would become "adults" in the faith.

Catholic religious education for those preparing for Confirmation still emphasizes reception of the seven gifts of the Spirit. The seven gifts are not the problem. Rather, it is the idea that these are only received through the sacrament of Confirmation that is problematic.

Such thinking is thoroughly dualistic, as if the Spirit is somewhere else and only "comes" when the right words and gestures are invoked by a bishop. It is a clear denial of a Divine Presence permeating all of creation. It calls into question the baptismal affirmation of the Spirit's presence in the child. It also is quite contrary to Jesus' preaching that the Spirit is always present with us. The presence of the Spirit of God is freely given; it is essential to existence. It is not dependent on a particular ritual and people with special powers to access the Spirit.

The best contemporary approach to Confirmation, if it is to remain a sacrament in its own right, is to understand it as an affirmation of the Divine Presence. Children preparing for Confirmation should still learn about the "gifts" of the Spirit. They should reflect on and discuss where and in whom these gifts have been and are clearly expressed in our world. They should reflect on how they themselves give expression to the gifts of the Spirit. Which "gift" do they think is strongest in them? Which gifts are most evident in their parents? In their brothers and sisters? They could be encouraged to tell their parents and their brothers and sisters how they see the gifts of the Spirit present and active in their lives.

How is the Spirit best expressed in their particular class? In friends? In the teacher?

Teachers, parents, grandparents and sponsors should approach Confirmation time resolving to affirm the presence of the Spirit in the child's life. Each parent and each grandparent, for example, could write a letter to the child being confirmed along the lines, *"Dear Amy, I want to tell you how I see the Spirit of God in your life and how much I treasure you for the ways you show that Spirit.*

I love the way you ... On your Confirmation Day I will celebrate with great joy the gift you are to your family and friends. You are so precious to all of us ..."

Surely the child would be wonderfully affirmed and delighted to receive such letters.

Prayer for a class or a child preparing for Confirmation

We give thanks for the Spirit of God

in our world

and in all people.

We give thanks for the people

who show us what the Spirit of God can do

when they allow the Spirit to work in their lives.

We give thanks for their wisdom,

for their care and concern for others,

for their generosity and courage,

and for the many ways they make the world a better place.

We give thanks for the Spirit of God in our lives,

in our own particular gifts and abilities.

May we use our own gifts of the Spirit well

so that God's Spirit will be seen in all we do and say. Amen.

Reconciliation

Who is hurt by sin? God? No. Not unless we think of God as a deity shaped by our images of person and then imagine that this God reacts to the misdemeanours of the human species.

People are hurt by sin. The environment is hurt by sin. Only to the extent that God comes to expression in people and in the natural world can we speak of God being hurt by sin.

Reconciliation, then, should not focus on a personal God who is hurt by sin, or whether that God forgives us or not, or who has special powers to forgive in God's name. It should avoid prayers addressed to that God saying how sorry we are to have offended "Him". Reconciliation should focus on who or what has been hurt by our greed, our pride, our selfishness and any other ways we do harm.

In recent years Church authority in the Vatican, aware of the significant decline in the regular use of this sacrament by mainstream Catholics, has reiterated the essential role of the priest as the only person who can forgive on behalf of God and the Church community. The Vatican's ongoing concern seeks to uphold the role of the priest rather than seeking to understand why so many Catholics have moved away from the confessional for their experience of reconciliation. These Catholics have sensed, even without articulating what is happening, that reconciliation has more to do with people interacting with one another than with a priest absolving them. They have sensed that the Divine is not confined to operating within Church rituals and structures.

For children the focus in the reconciliation process should firstly be on reciprocity: *how would you feel if someone acted like that towards you.* This is the language they can understand. The sacrament of reconciliation invites children to reflect on how their behavior causes disharmony, hurt or distress within a class, among friends, within a family or to the environment. We should then help them to express sorrow for hurting other people or destroying property or for disturbing harmony and trust.

The liturgy should be a celebration, not a ritual that weighs heavily on children's minds. Traditionally the sacrament has celebrated God's readiness to forgive us unconditionally if we are genuinely sorry. The shift now is to celebrate that we are ready to forgive one another and that other people are ready to forgive us. This is how God forgives – in and through us. It is also a celebration of forgiveness itself: to forgive and to be forgiven are both re-energizing for the human spirit.

Any ritual of reconciliation should emphasize the Divine here present and active within and among the participants. The ritual can be conducted with or without a priest.

The following Reconciliation prayer is adapted for children from *"Reconciliation – A Different Sense of Sin"* in *Praying a New Story.*

It should follow classroom discussion about why we have this ritual and a quiet reflection time for children to think about what they are sorry for.

Ω: Reconciliation Prayer

We believe that the Spirit of God present all throughout the universe

is present with us, every day of our lives.

In us, the Spirit of God can be

generous,

loving,

creative,

happy,

delighted,

sad,

and disappointed.

God loves in us;

God laughs in us;

God cries in us;

God cares through us.

We give thanks for Jesus

who opened our minds

to this understanding of who we are.

We give thanks for all the people

who have taught us

and shown us

how to live in ways that help one another.

We express our sorrow

for the times we have not behaved as we should,

especially for the ways that we have hurt other people.

We are sorry for any rudeness we may have shown to others;

We are sorry for any selfishness

and for any refusal to be generous.

We will do our best to let God's Spirit be seen in whatever we do and say and in our care for others.

We make this prayer in the name of Jesus who was always ready to forgive people who hurt him.

Amen.

Ideally, there should be some gesture to follow the prayer, for example, a sign of peace in which the children are aware they are expressing forgiveness to one another and to others and that they, in turn, are being forgiven by others.

Eucharist

The earlier section on Holy Thursday lays the foundation for understanding and appreciating the Eucharist and should be read as background to the following reflections.

In June 2001 the United States Conference of Catholic Bishops issued a statement on The Real Presence of Jesus Christ in the Sacrament of the Eucharist: Basic Questions and Answers. In #13 the Statement acknowledges that "Christ is present" in the person of the priest, in the Word, in the assembled people and in other sacraments, but the way in which Christ is present in the consecrated bread "surpasses the others". This presence in the consecrated bread is called "real", says the statement, not to exclude the idea that the other forms of presence are "real" too, "but rather to indicate presence par excellence, because it is substantial…" Earlier, in #4, the statement says that "in order for the whole Christ to be present – body, blood, soul and divinity – the bread and wine cannot remain, but must give way so that his glorified Body and Blood may be present. Thus in the Eucharist the bread ceases to be bread in substance…"

This one-sided focus on the bread that no longer remains bread but is mysteriously changed into a different substance is an unfortunate aspect of traditional Catholic teaching on the Eucharist. It results in the consecrated bread becoming an object to be analysed and venerated as *the* place above all other places or objects where the Sacred Presence resides. This approach needs to be counterbalanced by several considerations. First, it does not fit in any way with the Jewish meal on which this sacrament is founded and the way symbols were and still are used in that meal. Second, it places undue emphasis on the bread as sacred rather than on the people. Jesus would surely be surprised at that. Third, it emphasizes reception rather than commitment. Fourth, it has led to a long history of dependence on priests with their special power to access the Sacred for the Church community.

None of this is likely to change greatly in our lifetime. It is certain that Church leadership in Rome and bishops throughout the world will not countenance any questioning of the Eucharistic tradition. However, there is another way of understanding the Eucharist that is more faithful to Jesus and his intent at his last meal and which can greatly enrich appreciation of what the Eucharist is really about. This approach shifts from focusing on the bread as object to be received to focusing on the Eucharist as a ritual that affirms our own sacredness and challenges us to give our "Amen" to *being* the Body of Christ. This is what we saw in reflecting on Holy Thursday: the central issue in Eucharistic thought and practice should be whether we will say "Yes" to following what Jesus asks of us, rather than what we believe about the consecrated bread. On the night before he died, Jesus was seeking commitment from his followers when he broke bread and shared it with them. Commitment was the issue then and it should be now, not reception

We are not likely to escape the traditional emphasis on the bread as sacred object but we can try to counterbalance that emphasis. If we understand the words of St Augustine, written sixteen hundred years ago (quoted in Chapter Two), we will surely develop for ourselves and for children a most enriching appreciation of the Eucharist: *we* are the Body of Christ; it is *our mystery* that is placed on the Lord's table; we receive *our mystery*; we reply

"Amen" to *that which we are*; we receive what *we are*.

When preparing children for First Communion or when teaching about the sacrament we should keep this early tradition in mind. We need to make clear that the "Amen" given in response to "The Body of Christ" should never be confined to an expression of belief about Real Presence in the consecrated bread. Children should be led to believe that their Amen is saying Yes to their own desire to live and act as they believe Jesus would want them to. Their Amen is saying Yes: they are bearers of the Sacred Presence and they will show that in the way they relate with other people.

Surely we would not want future generations of Catholics to be deprived of this rich understanding of the Eucharist as most Christian adults today have been.

Children should not be expected to understand "Body of Christ" terminology in its theological sense. They need to understand what it means for them in everyday life: Yes, we are good people; Yes, we will live and behave as good people.

There is another tradition, long pushed into the background because of the emphasis on priestly power alone being able to consecrate the bread. This neglected tradition is being recovered and brought into practice today. It has its roots in the Acts of the Apostles (2:46), *They met in their houses for the breaking of bread; they shared their food gladly and generously*. In accord with this practice of the early followers of Jesus, people meet in their houses, share food, tell stories and break bread in memory of Jesus. There is no need for a priest to preside at such gatherings since there is no thought of consecrating the bread into a different reality. Instead, the focus is on the bread as symbol, on remembering Jesus' willingness to die for what he believed and on the participants' willingness to ritualize, through the sharing of bread and wine, their commitment to allowing the Spirit that moved in Jesus' life to move freely in their lives.

The following home liturgy respects this earliest custom of the followers of Jesus who gathered to break and eat bread.

Ω: Home Liturgy

Leader:

We gather in the belief

that God's Spirit, present throughout all the universe,

is here present in us,

in ... (name everyone present).

All:

We give thanks for the ways God's Spirit

is seen in who we are and what we do.

(Take a few minutes and allow each person to share how he or she has seen God's Spirit active in other family members in recent days. For example, mother to seven year old daughter: "Mary, I really appreciated the way you helped me to clean the house on Saturday. That was very thoughtful of you.")

All:

We give thanks for Jesus and the way God's Spirit was expressed in his life:

(Family members could read each of these statements in turn)

- *when he helped sick people*

- *when he blessed children*

- *when he cured blind people*

- *when he told people that God was always close to them*

- *when he taught people never to fear God*

- *when he asked people to love one another*

We remember that the night before he died, Jesus had a meal with his friends.

He asked them to keep on believing that God was always close to them.

He broke the bread ...

(Break the bread in silence. Let this be a deliberate ritual action so that attention is focused on it. After the bread is broken, someone reads:)

This broken bread reminds us of Jesus giving everything for what he believed.

We eat this bread now, silently and reverently, in memory of Jesus.

We eat it knowing that the same Spirit that moved in Jesus is present in our living and loving.

Let us eat together now and say Yes to the Spirit of Love in our lives.

(After everyone has finished eating, someone reads)

Jesus and his friends drank wine at the meal.

We drink now to celebrate we are family and friends bonded in the Spirit of God.

As we drink together let it be our way of saying we will allow the Spirit of Love to be seen in all we do and say.

(After everyone has finished, pause for a short time, before continuing.)

Everyone read together:

We give thanks for all that has been

and for all we are for each other as family and friends.

May the bonds of our loving

grow stronger and stronger.

May we always be for each other, for other people and for our world,

people who allow God's Spirit to be seen in all we do and say.

Amen.

Chapter Eight

On Being Christian: A Reflection for Christian Educators.

Adult educators who try to implement the suggestions in this book may face strong opposition from conservative believers and the charge that they are no longer entitled to call themselves "Christian". The opposition will come from those bishops, clergy and Christian laity who consider that unquestioning fidelity to traditional Christian doctrine is essential to being "truly" Christian.

This raises the question: What really constitutes being "Christian"?

Is it primarily allegiance to institutional Church authority and to belief in official Christian doctrine?

Is that what being a Christian is really about?

Is it like being a member of a club that has rules and laws and beliefs and if you do not like those rules and laws and beliefs, well, look elsewhere because you obviously no longer belong there?

Many Christians struggling with traditional belief have heard, "You cannot call yourself a Christian any more if you do not believe ... (this or that)".

Usually the "this or that" has nothing to do with Jesus' preaching about God-with-us.

It is as if we have two sets of railway tracks to represent Christian faith.

One track, representing Jesus' preaching about God's presence in people's lives, goes just a few miles before being diverted into a siding.

The other track, representing the Christian religion with all its doctrines, practices and biblical fundamentalism, is the longer, more important track and has numerous smaller tracks branching from it.

Many Christians would reject the suggestion, clearly implied here, that Jesus' preaching about the Divine Presence in our living and loving is generally not considered an essential characteristic of Christian identity.

In thought and practice, however, there *are* two separate railway tracks in operation and they are miles apart in their direction and intent. Only one of them, sometimes couched in terms of "being faithful to the Church's teaching", is typically used to determine what makes anyone a Christian.

So let us examine these tracks to see why they are not intersecting.

As highlighted throughout this book, Jesus' basic message is inclusive and universal. The mystery we call "God" is intimately present to every human person, regardless of race, gender, religion or occupation. Jesus opened eyes and minds to the unseen reality of human existence: we live in the mystery we call "God" and this Divine Presence comes to visible expression in human loving. We do not need people with special power to access God's presence. Rather, Jesus urged us to reflect on our everyday living and loving and come to awareness of the wonder of God-with-us.

This is good news that all people can understand because it is the language of human experience. It is the religious insight that can be, and should be, brought anew to every age as understanding and knowledge of our universe and of our place in it change.

A religion professing to keep alive Jesus' insight would be expected to promote it for all people to hear. It would be expected that the task of preaching this insight would be at the very heart of this religion's identity and mission. It would also be expected that personal fidelity to believing, living and spreading this teaching of Jesus would be *the* critical factor in determining whether someone who belonged to this religious group was a faithful follower of Jesus.

But such is not the case.

Being a faithful follower of Jesus and his message is not the criterion used by institutional leadership and other equally conservative Christians to determine whether someone is "Christian" or not. It is of little or no concern to them. They use quite different criteria, based on doctrinal formulations and traditional practices stemming from those doctrines, to judge whether someone is a "true Christian". They use their theological mind-set to silence or control questioning voices, all the while ignoring the essential message of Jesus.

So how, when and why did Christianity evolve into a religious institution that shifted focus from Jesus' dream of revealing the kingdom of God in our midst?

The answer is clear. Jesus preached the accessibility of God-with-us for anyone who lives in love. Ignoring this central theme of Jesus' message, the institutional Church within one hundred years of Jesus' death, and following its break with the Jewish religion, focused almost exclusively on accessibility to an elsewhere God only through belief in Jesus and membership of the Church. It claimed a monopoly on access to God. This gave the fledgling institution a unique, watertight identity.

Christianity consequently immersed itself in doctrine and liturgy and prayer forms based on the premise that Jesus is the unique re-connector to an elsewhere Deity.

Belief in this theological schema and all of its ramifications, such as who Jesus had to be in order to access heaven for us, then became the test whether someone was truly "Christian" or not.

This is a form of institutional mind-control for the institution's sake. "Christian" in this context is not a word pointing to Jesus and the universality of his message. It is a word used to identify someone in accord with institutional belief that Jesus' primary role was to win access to or friendship with an elsewhere Deity. "Jesus saves us!" is the rallying cry of people embedded in this theological mind-set. Only Jesus can get us into heaven where this Deity lives. Furthermore, claims the *Catechism of the Catholic Church,* "To reunite all his children, scattered and led astray by sin, the Father willed to call the whole of humanity together into his Son's Church." (#845)

It is not surprising that this "Christian" identity is facing a crisis today. Many Christians no longer give credence to the image of God that underpins this theology.

Their notion of God expanded beyond anything they could ever have imagined when they were exposed to knowledge about the size and age of this universe. And when they bring to this knowledge their belief that the Divine Presence is everywhere, holding and sustaining everything in existence, questions arise in their minds about the Christian doctrinal notion of a Deity who oversees, listens, plans, intervenes and chooses only one group of people to be "His people". More questions arise when they are expected to believe that this Deity has very definite ideas on issues such as homosexuality or whether women should be ordained priests and that institutional leadership can infallibly tell them what this God thinks. Respect for institutional religion's regard for truth, honesty and integrity suffer when institutional leadership decrees that the questions which arise are not allowed to be discussed publicly and severely punishes theologians and other members of the Church if they do so.

These Christians are no longer willing to attend worship services that bear the language and imagery of a story and a concept of God they have left behind. They do not want to abandon their faith. When they turn to Jesus' preaching about God's presence with people, they see teaching that is compatible with and good news in today's worldview. They want to bring the wonderful insights of Jesus to contemporary knowledge about our universe. They are certainly not being unfaithful to Jesus and his message. Yet they are often branded as being unfaithful to "the Church" or not being "Christian".

Who is being unfaithful to Jesus here?

Who is really trying to bring the teaching of Jesus to this age?

187

The present crisis of belief mirrors a tension that has existed throughout Christian history: on the one hand, the mystics who stressed intimacy with God and the interconnectedness of all things in God; on the other hand, theologians and Church hierarchy who stressed correct thinking and used that theology to articulate the true "marks" or identifying elements of the Church. The mystics looked for and encountered the Divine Presence everywhere. Christian theology and Church officialdom focused on a God who can only be encountered through baptism and membership of the Church.

A more contemporary expression of the crisis is found among people who openly profess to be "spiritual" but want nothing to do with institutional religion. The vast majority of youth today as well as many life-long adult Christians find themselves in this category.

Christianity must engage the contemporary worldview if it is to accomplish its real goal of bringing to people the liberating, good news of Jesus as revealer of God-with-us. While institutional Christian leadership stays locked into protecting the Fall-redemption, elsewhere God theology, as if its identity depended on it, the task of educating children into a believable, expansive, inclusive Christian faith vision of life will necessarily fall to parents, grandparents and teachers who are prepared to step outside the traditional theological worldview and discover a far better story about God and Jesus and ourselves. It may be a challenging and thankless task, but the future vitality of "the Church" – people called to gather around and spread the "good news" revealed in Jesus – depends on people today being willing to engage the task. Praying "a new story" with children is the best gift we adult educators can offer the future Church.